RED PLUSH AND TROMBONES

Charles Dyer

RED PLUSH AND TROMBONES

The Lonely Trilogy

OBERON BOOKS
LONDON

WWW.OBERONBOOKS.COM

First published in 2011 by Oberon Books Ltd
521 Caledonian Road, London N7 9RH
Tel: +44 (0) 20 7607 3637 / Fax: +44 (0) 20 7607 3629
e-mail: info@oberonbooks.com
www.oberonbooks.com

A catalogue record for this book is available from the British
Library.

ISBN: 978-1-84943-039-5

Cover design by James Illman

Printed in Great Britain by CPI Antony Rowe, Chippenham.

Contents

PREFACE

My Trilogy grew from the life I led, the folk I knew, the things we said. I was an office-boy when Hitler's Heinkels were vomiting bombs upon Manchester and, night-times, I earned a-bob-or-two calling *'Beginners'* at a variety theatre up-the-road. Sixpence, you got, running errands, threepence ferrying gins to soft-shoe-shufflers, and twopence-a-go garnering 'phone-books for the *World's Strongest Woman* to shred. Magic! – albeit less titillating than an adolescent might have wished because of our ex-mothballed oldstagers keeping up the Curtain for lusty youngsters gone to War.

A pipsqueak, I was, among podgy baritones on the *Road to Mandalay* with dog-acts and aching acrobats. We had comely Chorus Lines but even the fluffiest chicks seemed too knowing, and the rest were resuscitated hens reminiscent of my Auntie Maggie all tummy-and-bottom in feathers. I relished calling the hours and delivering flowers to maidens but squirmed over fetching corn-plasters and senna pods for slightly-elderly dancing women. And I blushed when, in lieu of sixpences, they clasped my peach cheeks to their generous bosoms:

'Ee, couldn't you just eat him!' … *'Give us* a *kiss, cupcake –'*

– like diving into a jam-butty. Nice ladies, even so; hearts big as their thighs, although my mother would have died at some of their unappetizing dressing spaces. Lip-sticky mirrors. *Ugg-ugg* cotton wool. Knickers-festooned gas brackets. Fag ends in *Vaseline* lids, and flung stockings coiled into little French hats out of Victor Hugo. You felt very Bohemian backstage. Acrid tang of size on canvas. Sliding trombones in *Franz Lehár,* and the twice-nightly *whoomph* from a rumbustious crowd. Magic.

Beginners, please! My voice broke at that dear old Theatre. *Beginners, please!*

During one exciting Second House – in a shoe-box behind a ladder to the Flies, I found the abandoned repertoire of a departed Ham: three tattered issues of *Dick's Penny Plays.* Plays that *Dick* once published for a penny. Ditching Lord Lytton's *Richelieu* and Tolstoy's *Root of All Evil,* I tested my tongue on the Bard's *Hamlet* – with that belly-tickle excitement that spirals to your throat. *Hamlet* swept me from backside-dark to front of tabs. I became an actor, humbly at first: five shillings for reciting soliloquies on variety evenings in Manchester pubs.

And I saw my name in Lights (pinned under the dartboard) or chalked on slate behind the bar:

Charlie Dyer
in
Sandwiches With Shakespeare.

I performed *'To be or not to be'* in the voices of Winston Churchill and Others of our Day. Donning a Hitler moustache, knotted hanky on head and with rolled-up trousers – God and the Bard forgive me! – I rehashed the Master's wilting Prince into hoarse Plumber:

To diddle or not to diddle, that is the question:
Whether 'tis richer in the Bank to bolster
The drips and air-locks of advantageous faucets,
Or to chance-your-arm in a froth of bubbles,
And by overcharging, mend 'em.

For an encore I stuffed a pillow up Hamlet's jumper: *To burp or not to burp, that's indigestion. ...* Grovelling apologies. I was only fifteen a hundred years ago. Blame *Dick's Penny Plays!*

So much for the actor, but whence the playwright? *Nobody knows.* My great-grandma Mary Anne Dyer tumbled off *Llantysilio Mountain,* a spinster-mother banished by clamp-chinned elders. She could neither read nor write, and died in a workhouse. But perhaps – just perhaps, my Welsh Mary Anne is whispering through the tap-tap-tap of these keys? I hope so. Assuredly my first play was born out of high skies beyond the blue yonder – in the Royal Air Force. Midsummer 1944. Navigator, I was. 512 Squadron. We dropped Paratroop-lads on D-Day and towed Glider-boys to Arnhem. On a later posting to the Pacific, we flew weapons to the Islands, jeeps, ammunition, supplies, and I scribbled dialogue throughout long hauls from New Guinea across Borneo to Saigon. I scribbled through ten thousand miles over jungles and tropical atolls from Cancer to Capricorn, and finished my first play over the Philippines with a mildly rude Curtain Line – not quite a real word, a rhyme to one, but so hysterically funny that I giggled five hours across China Seas to Hong Kong.

Back to England in peace and quiet skies, I joined Pop Barlow's *Repertory Players* at Wednesbury Hippodrome in the Midlands where factory fields were browned by rusting swarf: no lush hibiscus nor sapphire pools, but honey-blest our audiences, warm stomping folk who cheered that first play of mine. I was director and juvenile lead in springtime 1948.

Having dipped my toe in provincial puddles, I left on itchy feet for deeper waters and into decades of touring the provinces. Acting; picking up West End crumbs; acting and typing between houses or at the digs or, after the show, with theatre-cat and stage-door-key in ghostly dressing rooms to *clinks, clanks,* and *Mary-Anne's whispers.* Whilst tap-tapping my own works, I yack-yacked in two hundred other writers' plays at one hundred and fifty venues. Here is a family tree of the theatres I played:

Pier,

Royalty

Town Hall

The Victoria

Winter Gardens

Coliseum, Dolphin

Kemble, Royal Court

Alhambra, Forum, Savoy

Alma, Carlton and Whitehall

Princess & Two Prince of Wales

Granville, Yvonne Arnaud, Embassy

Playhouse, Intimate, Capitol & County

Three Civics and Five Arts and Six Pavilions

Marlowe, Wimbledon, Richmond and Crewe

Olympia, Devonshire Park and Pleasure Gardens,

A Cinema, Regent, two Gaietys, seven Theatres New,

The Lyceum, Seven Grands, Eight Palaces, Twelve Empires

And one dozen each of Opera Houses and Kings and Granadas

Thirteen lucky Hippodromes & Sixteen Theatres Royal.

&&&

&&&

&&&

&&&

&&&

&&&&&&&&

From all that red plush and those trombones, came a penny-Hamlet out of Mary-Anne through a jam-butty kiss across footlights to the gods. So many years of living and loving plays.

Beginners Please!

Charles Dyer, 2011

RATTLE OF A SIMPLE MAN

WARY FELLA AND WINKING GAL

Vivien Leigh inspired *Rattle of A Simple Man* in early summer 1940.

Hot-footing into my seventeenth year, I fell passionately for Miss Leigh's Scarlet O'Hara in *Gone With The Wind* and swore to write her a play: if Shakespeare could do it for *Dick's Penny Hamlet* so could Charlie for Sweet Scarlet. *Virgin Lad Meets Sassy Minx*. My Dad was a commercial traveller. I used his old Remington and typed for an eternity, my mind a-quiver, my tomorrow an unswerving arrow and my target – disaster! The wretched typewriter had no soul. Page-less, I pined for Scarlet through callow-fluff to whiskers. Then, in 1959, I re-tackled *Rattle* whilst acting Shylock in *The Merchant of Venice* at Bromley's New Theatre.

Older, wiser, I learned to thread my characters' hearts between their lines.

* * *

Rattle of A Simple Man opened to rave reviews at London's *Garrick* in 1962. We ran for a year; with equally exciting seasons in Paris at the Gaité Montparnasse. Our French title was *La Crecelle* – of which the late Harold Hobson wrote (*Sunday Times*): 'No English postwar play has run so successfully in Paris as *La Crecelle*.' By then we had productions in Berlin, Rome, and across the World. Everywhere – and in America, where we opened with a happy bang at Broadway's Booth Theatre during a blistering April in 1963.

I met Vivien Leigh in America, as thrilling for me as success-itself. On Easter Sunday our *Rattle* company bussed me to a Bluebook charity affair; *where* is a mystery. My fallible memory recalls a sumptuous chateau, sweeping lawns, terraces sparkling with socialites and a sprinkling of Broadway-babble. *Dahling, your new face is divine! Lordy-Lordy, how slim, dahling! ... My my, how dishy to see you in health and diamonds.* ... All shadows now, the faces that thrilled me on that Sunday, faces from Saturday mornings at the Fleapit. Danny Kaye was there; John Gielgud for England; Charles Boyer, they said, circulating amongst fine French furniture and flock wallpaper; wealth dripping like a sultan's sweat.

By 'ell, there's posh for you, bach, as my ancestors would have muttered in the Valley; *and flamin' 'ot under the arm, boyo, I'll tell you.*

'Hundred degrees in the Big Apple. Suave impresarios sweltered inside their wilting flannel. Programme-fanning matrons s-s-s-steamed, with little cherries oozing wax on their Easter bonnets.

Heated actors grumbled as actors do, with space-a-plenty for muck-raking at that Sugar Chateau: the vestibule could have housed a marching band, in place of which we had a lovely flower-power girl of long tresses and limbs with an ormolu-encrusted harp between grasshopper knees. Languid wits suggested she was plucking *Fleder-maus*. But I rather liked her.

Two candy-floss staircases curved from the foyer's marble acre-age to a meringue gallery, and there she was – Vivien Leigh! – me climbing one staircase, Scarlet O'Hara descending the other. She was surrounded by chattering courtiers, and missed hearing my call. I called again:

'Miss Leigh! Miss Leigh – !'

She looked around, then downwards through the years, that same Scarlet O'Hara from the Manchester Gaiety, front row. Sooty-kitten face. Quizzical. Lip-corners quirky.

' – I wrote *Rattle* for you, Miss Leigh.'

Scarlet O'Hara shook her head, smiling a teeny frown, wag-gling fingers at her ears.

'*Rattle of a Simple Man*. I wrote it – for you.'

Then Scarlet's courtiers hurried her away. Vivien Leigh only lived four more years.

So she never knew. Ah well! A myriad actors have graced my plays. I am proud of everyone. And to this day, someone some-where is performing *Rattle*.

Beginners please!

* * *

RATTLE OF A SIMPLE MAN

The Winking Gal is called CYRENNE
The Wary Fella's name is PERCY;
and briefly, RICARD is the Brother.

Michael Codron presented *'Rattle'*
at London's Garrick Theatre in September 1962
with Sheila Hancock and Edward Woodward, directed by
Donald McWhinnie.
Daniel Moynihan played the Brother.
(John Colin took over as PERCY in 1963)

* * *

Merrick & Codron presented *'Rattle'*
at New York's Booth Theatre in April 1963
with Tammy Grimes and Edward Woodward, directed by
Donald McWhinnie.
George Segal played the Brother.

* * *

La Gaite-Montparnasse presented '*Rattle'*
in Paris, September 1963, with
Jacqueline Gauthier and Claude Rich,
directed by Michel Fagadu.
Yves Arcanel played the Brother.

* * *

The Year is 1958.
A wintery Saturday night in CYRENNE's basement flat
somewhere in London. The Action is more or less continuous.

* * *

Originally presented in three Acts,
the author has now updated his play into two Acts
(with a curtain-fall in the second Act).

ACT ONE

Up strikes the music! The Curtain rises. The dark stage is Invaded by rays of lamplight that fall through a window to linger upon a silky-frilly double bed. Outside, we glimpse old brickwork, railings, and basement steps leading to the pavement above. The music fades ...

A car door slams. A taxi drives away. We see the legs of two persons descending the area steps. The legs pause halfway:

CYRENNE: *(Off.)* Steady, darling! My, they are awf'ly steep. Maybe you should wait until I've opened up. Or are you going to run out on me?

PERCY: *(Off.)* No! ... No, um, 'course not.

> *CYRENNE opens the front door, clicks a switch, and the Lighting brightens to reveal a pleasant bed-sitter with scullery-come-kitchen up steps on the side. CYRENNE sets her handbag here, her keys there, her gloves in a drawer, and so forth.*

CYRENNE: *(Calls.)* Well, come in, love!

> *CYRENNE (whose name rhymes with 'mirren'.) is neither a Lamplight Lil nor a golden hearted tart, nor does her voice scrape nor scratch. Her moods, on the other hand, are complex. In turn she is mocking or kindly, choosy or inviting, tempestuous or cold, earthy or prim. She is all these things.*

CYRENNE: *(Calls.)* Come along, Percy! I shan't eat you.

> *CYRENNE turns on the Kitchen lamp; lights the gas under a kettle, then returns to the bedroom window, and beckons:*

CYRENNE: Come along! The kettle's on. *(She closes the window curtains.)*

> *PERCY enters. He seems an ordinary fellow, late thirty-ish, forty-ish. He has comic phases, some conscious, some unconscious, but he knows only too well his limitations, and uses an intense pride, a rocky dignity to hide his sad fear that nobody wants or needs him. Above all, he is not an idiot!*

13

For this reason, both he and we must believe that CYRENNE is a real princess! Prudish Percy would run a mile from anyone less.

CYRENNE: Did you require a cup of tea, Percy?

PERCY: Er -no, I'm not bothered. Thanks all the same.

CYRENNE: Good! 'Saves gas. *(She turns it off.)*

(PERCY has been celebrating some sporting event, as we see, by his multicoloured scarf, rosette – and rattle. He is not drunk, however, just muzzy. Now, as CYRENNE busies herself in the kitchen, he takes in his surroundings and giggles to himself.)

PERCY: What a thing, eh! Jemima, what a – oogh. *(He sways slightly, placing a hand to his brow, and then, with much less bravado, adds.)* Streuth! What a thing!

(CYRENNE turns out the kitchen light and moves into the bedroom. She places her earrings and so forth on the dressing-table, then unzips her frock and steps out of it, wearing panties and a bra. PERCY is standing LC, clutching the rattle. He throws it on to the bed with a nervous laugh when CYRENNE looks at him. Then he thrusts his hands deep into his raincoat pockets and examines the carpet around his feet.)

Don't we sort of talk or anything?

CYRENNE: Why?

PERCY: Well, you know, I only thought, well, you know.

CYRENNE: *(Quizzically.)* Change of heart, love?

PERCY: *(Bravely.)* No! Not at all. I'm game for anything. *(He thrusts his hands even deeper into his pockets and edges half a step away.)*

CYRENNE: And anything goes, eh, love? *(She folds her arms.)* A spoonful of life; daring week-end in the wicked city?

PERCY: I've been in London before. Many times.

CYRENNE: Never done this before, though, have you!

PERCY: *(Defensively.)* Yes.

CYRENNE: Have you?

PERCY: Yes. 'Course I have!

CYRENNE: *(Smiling.)* Scouts' honour? Okey-doke. *(She slides across the bed to his side, and yelps humorously when she momentarily sits on the rattle. Now she helps him off with his raincoat and places it, with his scarf, on the chair L.)* Are you married?

PERCY: Um-no.

CYRENNE: *(Looking at him.)* No, you're not. Go on! I shan't look.

(She turns down the coverlet; and, without looking, passes the rattle to him.)

Who won, incidentally?

PERCY: Oh, don't ask! It was horrible. I reckon somebody covered the ball in grease; and as for the teams, they were so dead they should've carried flowers.

(Silence for awhile. CYRENNE turns down the right-hand side of the bedclothes. PERCY sneaks a look at her.)

Of course, the ground was too hard. Frosty. *(He clears his throat.)*

CYRENNE: *(Looking up at him.)* Don't be shy!

PERCY: I'm not! I've seen hundreds of women.

CYRENNE: I've seen hundreds of men.

PERCY: I suppose you must have, although you're not quite what I imagined – not at all. *(He takes his hands out of his pockets, then puts them back again.)*

(CYRENNE crosses to him.)

Few months ago, a gang of us were up in Morecambe. Phew! Saw a proper game there – only local teams ...

(His voice dies away as CYRENNE takes off his tie.)

CYRENNE: It's Percy, isn't it?

PERCY: Yes. Percy Winthram. I'm from Manchester.

CYRENNE: Mine's Cyrenne. I was down in Manchester once: on a modelling job for one of the big stores.

PERCY: It'd be Lewis's in Market Street.

CYRENNE: *(Placing his tie on the chair L.)* May go down again some time.

PERCY: Up! You go up to Manchester.

CYRENNE: Well, as long as you get there. *(He takes off his jacket.)* It's a nice suit.

PERCY: It's my best. S'quite good quality.

CYRENNE: *(With a sudden thought.)* You do have money?

PERCY: 'Course I have. Plenty.

CYRENNE: With you?

PERCY: Yes. I brought out thirty pounds this morning.

CYRENNE: You won't need all that, Percy, unless you're staying the week. *(She lays his jacket on the chair L, then crosses to the bed-end and sits to put on her slippers.)*

PERCY: I've to be back on Monday morning. Win or lose, I promised I'd take mother to ... *(He stops.)*

CYRENNE: *(Not unkindly.)* All have mothers, don't you! Behind every man is a Ma.

PERCY: Oh, that doesn't hold me back. I act like I please, don't worry! I'm – I'm thirty-five, you know.

CYRENNE: Oh, you must be-to have seen so many women. *(She watches him steadily.)*

(PERCY lowers his eyes to the floor and unfastens one shirt button. This takes ages.)

Would you rather I got ready first?

PERCY: No! No!

CYRENNE: One of us must make a move, dear. Take your pick!

PERCY: It – it just seems so cold-blooded like this.

CYRENNE: It's a matter of time, though, isn't it. We can't meet the family and go walks together. But I don't mind: nobody's forcing you to make love. If you prefer, I'll make a pot of tea and when you're ready you can scoot.

PERCY: I'm not ... *(He stops.)*

CYRENNE: Not what?

PERCY: Not – not paying for nothing.

CYRENNE: *(Rising; flashing.)* Now stop that, lovey! You pay for my time. I don't give a damn how you spend it; but you pay for it!

(She dons her black négligé from the hooks down L.)

PERCY: Oh, I feel umpty. I really do. *(He sits on the bed.)* I've a head like a rocket-tail at blast-off. Oooo – *(He lies full length.)*

CYRENNE: Well! What a come-down! Shaking his rattle; throwing his hat in the air! "See you tomorrow, lads! Don't tell mother: you'll make dad jealous! Up the Wrens!" Marvellous! *(Crossing up L, she locks the door and pockets the key.)* I get the cash; and you get the key.

PERCY: Could I have a glass of cold water, please?

CYRENNE: Everybody's Romeo! Read next week's sizzling instalment! Oh, lady, you do pick 'em. And don't be sick over my bed!

(She fills a glass of water from the kitchen tap.)

PERCY: *(Sitting up.)* I'm not that bad: glass of water and I'll be fine. Where did the rest of the lads go? Back to the digs?

CYRENNE: I've no idea; but you'd better think up some killerdiller tales: they're expecting great things from you.

(She hands him the glass of water.) Especially the one with red hair.

PERCY: That's Ginger – I mean, we call him Ginger. Did he go with the others?

CYRENNE: Maybe – after he fell off the taxi. *(She sits at her dressingtable.)* He hung on the back for half a mile, yelling merry hell.

PERCY: I'm sorry if I've caused you any inconvenience.

CYRENNE: S'al! part of the racket. *(Makes a note in her diary.)* "Nineteen Hundred and Fifty Eight. A.P."

PERCY: AP?

CYRENNE: After Percy. What's the time?

PERCY: Quarter past eleven. Why?

CYRENNE: Income tax. *(She grins, then gurgles merrily at his expression.)*

PERCY: Why do you do this sort of thing, Cyrenne?

CYRENNE: *(Brushing her hair.)* What sort of thing?

PERCY: Well – you know, live like you do. Oh, I imagine everyone asks you that.

CYRENNE: Usually bank managers who are writing plays; or Bible-punchers with helping hands – one of those calls every Thursday, with pale watery eyes, and begs to hear my problems. Oh, brother!

PERCY: He may be a kindly person who's genuinely interested in your welfare.

CYRENNE: *(Meekly.)* Yes, Percival: like the time he asked me to undress while he listened.

PERCY: Well, there was only genuine interest in my question. I'm not – not perverted or anything. I've no problems.

CYRENNE: *(Meaningly.)* No?

PERCY: Now listen, miss. It was you approached me. You spoke to me in that club. You suggested this.

CYRENNE: *(Shrugging.)* It didn't stop you coming.

PERCY: Only because I was merry. I was a bit merry. And now, if you must know, I'm very ashamed.

CYRENNE: *(Flinging down her hair brush.)* Oh, you're ashamed!

PERCY: Yes. I feel awful about it.

(CYRENNE rises angrily. She goes for PERCY's jacket, scarf and raincoat and hurls them on to the bed; then returns to her stool R.)

CYRENNE: You're breaking my heart. Run and tell "the lads" all about your naughty night!

PERCY: You have the door-key.

(CYRENNE throws the key on the floor and continues brushing her hair.)

Um – how er – how much do I pay?

CYRENNE: Auntie doesn't rob schoolboys. Leave a shilling and a piece of string on the mantelpiece.

PERCY: Why are you so peeved? *(He rises, bends to look for the key; and quickly flops down again. He rubs the back of his head, with a groan.)*

Oh-don't keep brushing your hair! Must you?

CYRENNE: Oh, rich. *(She drops the brush and swings round.)* Are we married now or something? Whatever would your mummy say?

PERCY: It was scratching the backs of my eyes.

(CYRENNE makes a sound of amusement. She rises, then hands him the glass of water from the floor by his feet.)

CYRENNE: Shall you tell mother all about your naughty night?

PERCY: No.

CYRENNE: Aw! What about the "lads"? *(She imitates his accent on "lads".)* Shall you tell the lads?

PERCY: Probably.

CYRENNE: Everything? Exactly as it happened – at quarter past eleven in Nineteen-Hundred-and-Fifty-Eight?

PERCY: I suppose so.

CYRENNE: It won't be very exciting, will it! Yes, I can just see that pub in Manchester tomorrow night. Yup! *(She slaps her thigh.)* There's Ginger an' Chalky an' Fred-and there's you in the middle, looking ashamed. "Eeee, I was so ashamed, Ginger," says Percival. And Ginger says, "Eeee, I'm proud you were ashamed, Percival." Then all the gentlemen join hands and yell: "Good old Percy! Pass the Bible!"

PERCY: I must've offended you. I'm sorry if I did.

CYRENNE: *(Sitting beside him on the bed-end.)* What will you say about me?

PERCY: I'll say ... *(He changes his mind and sips water.)*

CYRENNE: *(Quietly.)* Yes, think about it. I often do-with fellows like you. Do they say, "I'm glad I didn't"-people like you, Percy? Or has the story grown by tomorrow? Dark brown chuckles and nudges in the ribs: "Ho, ho! What a night, chaps! What a night!"

(PERCY sips his water doggedly; but she nudges him.)

Percy?

PERCY: We-ell – *(rising, he puts his tumbler on the table down L.)* you see, I've never talked about things of – well, with a lady. I mean, you're so brassy with it.

CYRENNE: Won't you be brassy with Ginger?

PERCY: That's between men.

CYRENNE: And this is between people. Aren't men people?

PERCY: Yes, but – oh! D'you have an aspirin handy?

CYRENNE: *(Moving up R to the tallboy.)* You still haven't told me how I come off in the expurgated edition. You know, the one you'll be so ashamed of.

PERCY: *(Hotly.)* Very well, I'll tell them the truth. I'll say I'm no good; I'm a flop. Satisfied?

CYRENNE: Then you've no call to be ashamed. *(She finds a bottle of aspirins in a tallboy drawer and brings them to him.)*

PERCY: There is a path between my ears full of little men with hammers. *(He sits down L and takes aspirins with a sip of water.)*

(CYRENNE drops a packet of cigarettes on the table beside him.)

CYRENNE: Help yourself.

PERCY: No, thanks. I'm all smoked out. You know, you're a strange one, Cyrenne. I come here to – well, to – and end up with some kind of lecture.

CYRENNE: I'm intelligent, do you mind? *(She moves C.)* It so happens I've travelled the world and I speak three languages. I passed through college with honours. I'm an M.A.– if you wish me to boast.

PERCY: That's very good. Very good indeed.

CYRENNE: My father was a brigadier in the army. I was raised among people like that. Thirty pounds! I've spent more than your thirty pounds on – on a hat. *(Grandly.)* Or a sudden whim, believe me!

PERCY: Don't reckon any hat's worth thirty pounds. *(He rises; then meanders to the kitchen stairs, rubbing his hands briskly.)* I didn't half drink some stuff tonight. Phew! I wondered if, um – *(He stops.)* I wondered if...

CYRENNE: *(Lounging on the bed.)* What, love?

PERCY: Nothing. *(He peers into the kitchen.)* Is that a cupboard or something?

CYRENNE: *(Smiling faintly.)* No.

PERCY: Oh. *(He meanders back to his chair.)*

CYRENNE: *(Blandly.)* Why?

PERCY: Nothing. I just wondered.

CYRENNE: I own this house: bought the mortgage. If I wished I could move upstairs. Just haven't bothered.

PERCY: You're lucky. Wish I owned a house. *(He moves up L, opens the door, and looks into the small corridor beyond. Then he closes the door, returns down L, and points to the door down L.)* Another room in there?

CYRENNE: *(Twinkling.)* Yes.

PERCY: Bathroom, is it?

CYRENNE: No. *(She lies back on the bed.)*

PERCY: Oh. *(He rubs his hands.)*

CYRENNE: It's for luggage and odds and ends. A kind of dressing-room. There's a bathroom on the other side of it.

PERCY: Oh! Would you excuse me, please.

> *(PERCY exits down L, rubbing his hands. CYRENNE laughs to herself and rises. Picking up the key, she is about to replace it in the front door; then she pauses, weighing it thoughtfully in her hands. On an impulse she moves to the dressing-table and puts it in a powder bowl. Now she takes the rosette from PERCY's raincoat and pins it on her dressing-gown. She admires the effect in her mirror; then puts his scarf round her neck, collects his rattle from the tallboy and moves c, twirling it. PERCY re-enters down L.)*

PERCY: You could have said straight away.

CYRENNE: You could have asked straight away.

PERCY: It's not the sort of thing a gentleman does. *(He puts on his tie.)*

CYRENNE: Up in Manchester.

PERCY: Anywhere.

CYRENNE: Oh, we do it all the time in London.

PERCY: You're just trying to make me look silly. You've been acting clever ever since I came. I admit I was wrong – somewhere along the line; but you did invite me here in the first place. *(He dons his jacket and throws his raincoat over a shoulder.)* Could I have my things, please?

(CYRENNE gives him the scarf and rattle, then pats the rosette.)

CYRENNE: Souvenir for Cyrenne?

PERCY: Mm? Oh. Yes. Yes, please have it. Oh – I'm not quite sure what we decided – with regard to terms.

(CYRENNE ponders with assumed gravity.)

CYRENNE: Oh, I think all details being taken into consideration and with due regard to the culminating factors, we may safely assume – it's on the house!

PERCY: *(Laughing uncertainly.)* Oh. Thank you very much.

CYRENNE: Not at all. *(She waves her hand in the air and lies back on the bed.)*

PERCY: Well! I've enjoyed our little chat. *(He moves hesitantly to the door and turns.)* I, er – I may not be up in London again for some while.

CYRENNE: Down!

PERCY: Pardon? Oh, yes: down in London. Been quite exciting – everything and all. And thanks for the glass of water and the aspirins. I can see that you're, um – well, a very nice kind of person.

CYRENNE: Underneath it all.

PERCY: No! I mean it! I've never talked to anyone quite so interesting. You don't meet many girls that are – that are, you know, original. And you are! Anyway... *(He moves to the door up L and pauses quite a while with his hand on the door-knob. Then he comes back to CYRENNE, who is lying with her head hanging over the end of the bed and following a pattern on the carpet with her fingers.)* You don't suppose

Ginger could've – no, you say he fell off the taxi. *(He goes back to the door, then returns with a fresh thought.)* Some of the other lads, though – maybe they're hanging around – waiting to see how I got on. Could be, you know. And – well, I've been so – so quick. You see?

CYRENNE: But we've nothing to be ashamed of – have we?

PERCY: Oh – no. No. *(He moves to the door, then turns again.)* I er – I work in a cotton mill back home: in the Research Department, testing different tensilities; working on improved fabrics, you know. Nothing exactly scientific, but, um – are you listening?

CYRENNE: Yes.

PERCY: *(Moving down.)* Hey! D'you know, I might've had something to do with that very dressing-gown you're wearing.

CYRENNE: *(Gravely.)* Sort of makes you stop and want to think.

PERCY: Yes. *(He shakes his head sadly.)* You know, Cyrenne, we come down here every year; and yet – once Saturday's finished, it's always dead for me. And tomorrow there's only the coach station – cold, early and Sunday-ish; chaps bragging about the women they've met, the beer they've drunk; then the long drive home with a headache. Not that I'm grumbling, you understand! There's always the girl-friend, you know. Oh, I've a very nice girlfriend. Oh, yes. I'm a happy man. I'm a very happy man. *(He looks at his watch.)* Ee, you'll never guess the time

CYRENNE: Oh yes I could! It's half-past Never.

PERCY: Aw, give over! Look – I'm not begging favours; but c-could – couldn't I stay a bit longer? – as a friend – j-just to talk?

(CYRENNE raises her head and looks at him. Then suddenly she swings off the bed and moves to the tallboy up R. From a drawer

she takes a blouse. Throwing off her dressing-gown, she puts on the blouse. Then she says.)

CYRENNE: I may have people calling.

PERCY: Oh. Oh, I see.

CYRENNE: My sister and her husband.

PERCY: *(More brightly.)* Oh.

CYRENNE: He's a brilliant surgeon. They often call in for an hour. Sometimes they bring a whole crowd and we have a party. My sister's husband is very large – much broader than you, and he's tall with it. Nice man. I like him. Always decent with me. They're charming people, all of them. *(She takes the rosette from her dressing-gown and holds it against her blouse, surveying herself in the mirror.)*

PERCY: They sound very nice. Very nice.

CYRENNE: They're not bound to call. 'Tisn't a definite arrangement. No! Doesn't match the blouse! *(She throws the rosette into a waste-basket and hurries out of the door down L.)*

PERCY: Hey! That was meant as a keepsake: not to be thrown away. *(He crosses to the waste-basket and retrieves his rosette.)* I'll have it back, seeing you're so pernickety. *(He moves to the door down L and shouts.)* Best of luck to you, anyway! *(He strides to the door up L, stops, then walks slowly back again. Shouting.)* I'll be off then. O.K.? Are you listening?

(CYRENNE reappears suddenly, wearing skin-tight black trousers. She goes to the dressing-table and picks up her diary.)

What if they don't call?

CYRENNE: Someone's always popping in.

PERCY: You're not – going out again?

CYRENNE: No. *(She lies on the bed, with her toes on the pillow, and reads her diary.)*

PERCY: Would you mind my stopping until somebody did call?

(CYRENNE sighs indifferently and turns a page.)

Would you?

CYRENNE: Would I what?

PERCY: *(Irritably.)* Can I stay until someone calls?

CYRENNE: Shouldn't you go to your hotel-or-whatever-it-is, and sober up?

PERCY: Who's drunk? I was never anything more than mellow, just a happy glow.

(CYRENNE turns another page.)

Aw, I'm so walked on I'm getting a matt finish! *(He strides huffily to the door up L, finds it locked, and strides back again. He paces the bed area, muttering darkly, and then goes on his knees to look under the bed-end.)*

(CYRENNE leans her head right over, close to his.)

CYRENNE: *(Innocently.)* Lost something?

PERCY: The key. You tossed it down. I can't see it.

CYRENNE: Hmm1 You'd better go through the window. *(She returns to her diary.)*

PERCY: Climb through?

CYRENNE: You could take a running jump.

PERCY: Through the window!

CYRENNE: Yes – open it first.

(PERCY goes to the window L.)

And bring back a locksmith.

PERCY: At this hour! All we need is to unscrew that plate. I could do it in five minutes if you've a screwdriver.

CYRENNE: D'you expect me to spend five minutes with a screwdriver each time anyone calls?

PERCY: Well, you threw it on the floor! *(He pulls aside the curtains.)*

Hey, there're bars on the window!

CYRENNE: Squeeze through!

PERCY: Squeeze ...! A python'd be hard pressed.

(CYRENNE flops back and, taking the weight on her shoulders, thrusts her legs up high. Then she does "developpes and entrechats" in the air.)

(Turning and watching her.) You have, um – you have a very nice figure.

CYRENNE: I'm glad you like it.

PERCY: Quite – quite nice hair, too.

(CYRENNE folds down into a sitting position. She smiles and nods towards the kitchen R.)

CYRENNE: Go put the kettle on!

PERCY: You mean ... ? Oh, thanks! *(He throws his rattle into the chair down L, and crosses eagerly to the kitchen.)* Yes, thank you very much. Ta. I'm most appreciative, I really am. *(He hangs his coat and scarf over the kitchen banisters.)* Be all right here, will it?

CYRENNE: *(Surveying it lazily.)* Move it – um, slightly to the left.

(PERCY does so, then stops.)

PERCY: Why?

CYRENNE: Oh, it'll probably be all right.

PERCY: You don't half say some odd things, you do really. *(He moves into the kitchen, turns on the light, and fills the kettle at the sink.)*

(CYRENNE rises and looks at herself in the dressing-table mirror. She smoothes her hands down her body.)

CYRENNE: There's a tin of biscuits above your head and some blue cheese. Shall we have that?

PERCY: Oogh, yes. I am a bit peckish. *(He reaches down the transparent plastic biscuit tin.)* Have you any more biscuits? There's only two.

CYRENNE: One each. Lovely!

PERCY: Oh. Yes.

(CYRENNE moves into the kitchen and stands watching as PERCY prepares a tray with cheese, biscuits, butter and so forth.)

CYRENNE: My family home had a huge stone-flagged kitchen. Oh, it was a mansion, really – in Hampshire. As a child I remember the daffodils reaching my waist; and my arms wouldn't meet around the great white pillars of the portico. A white gleaming mansion, and we called it "Old Wob". I couldn't count the servants we had – old Pickles the butler, old Ned the chauffeur ...

(PERCY is rinsing two cups under the tap.)

PERCY: I once stayed on a farm. Oh! I've wet your rent book.

(PERCY takes a rent book from its hook above the sink and hands it to her. CYRENNE places it on a shelf over the cooker.)

CYRENNE: It's not mine, but thank you. My father was such a handsome man – so distinguished. You had to respect as well as love him.

PERCY: I imagine everyone respects a brigadier. Is he dead, then?

CYRENNE: *(Nodding.)* He left all his money to my brother and me. My brother owns a country club.

PERCY: You're not half well connected! Was there much in the way of money? – if you'll pardon me asking.

CYRENNE: Ten thousand.

PERCY: *(Whistling.)* A small fortune.

CYRENNE: It soon goes.

PERCY: No doubt you spent a lot buying this house.

CYRENNE: No, a man bought this for me. *(She stretches against the wall.)* I could've had much more, but – well, you know.

PERCY: *(Disapproving.)* I see.

(The kettle whistles. CYRENNE turns off the gas.)

No! I'll do it.

CYRENNE: I'll serve up. You go and sit down. Go on!

(CYRENNE seems surprised. She backs away to the doorway.)

Go on! Scoot!

(CYRENNE walks meekly to the end of the bed and sits, waiting. PERCY pours water into the teapot.)

I must remember what mother's always saying: pot to the kettle, never kettle to the pot. Ooogh, marvellous. It'll run round the room, this tea. *(He throws a towel over his arm, waiter-fashion; takes the teapot in one hand, the tray in his other; turns off the light with his shoulder – and goes to sit beside CYRENNE.)* You know, I'm almost feeling healthy again. Must have been those aspirins. Mind you, my tongue still tastes like an old bath mat.

CYRENNE: Butter me a biscuit.

PERCY: Oh. All right. *(He does so.)* Do you have normal meals?

(CYRENNE bursts out laughing.)

What's up? What's the matter?

CYRENNE: No. They supply us with special food.

PERCY: I didn't mean it that way.

CYRENNE: Extra vitamins. Technicolored pills.

PERCY: I simply meant, well, some people – here's your biscuit.

CYRENNE: What about the cheese?

PERCY: Do your own cheese. You'll expect me to eat it next.

CYRENNE: *(Smiling.)* Sorry.

> *(PERCY butters his own biscuit, keeping his eyes to the task. CYRENNE bends her head down and looks at him.)*

Sorry, love.

PERCY: You've nothing to be sorry for. I'm not sulking, you know. I don't sulk.

CYRENNE: Here! *(She cuts him a piece of cheese.)*

PERCY: Ta. *(He takes it.)* You see, it's hard to think of something to say without a double meaning – in the circumstances, so to speak. And we are in – well – peculiar circumstances.

CYRENNE: *(Gravely.)* Oh, yes.

PERCY: I start to say something and all my sentences end in dots. When a character in a book sort of hesitates, you get dot-dot-dot-dot-dot. That's how I am.

CYRENNE: *(Nodding understandingly.)* It's horrid for you.

PERCY: I suppose I'm just – *(He giggles a little.)* just dotty. *(He laughs happily at this.)*

> *(CYRENNE smiles.)*

I always laugh at my own jokes. I'm the only one who does.

CYRENNE: Never mind.

> *(There is a longish pause while they munch their biscuits and cheese. Every so often he looks at her, then looks away when she returns his look.)*

PERCY: I hope I'm not keeping you up.

> *(CYRENNE shakes her head gravely, just managing not to laugh.)*

PERCY: Is your mother still alive?

CYRENNE: *(After a pause.)* No.

PERCY: Ah. Perhaps she died when you were very young, then?

CYRENNE: Yes. Yes, indeed. I was twelve.

PERCY: Did your dad look after you?

CYRENNE: We had a nanny.

PERCY: Oh, yes, of course.

CYRENNE: Father was always away fighting.

PERCY: Fighting who?

CYRENNE: *(Shrugging.)* He was away doing something.

PERCY: What regiment was your father, may I ask?

CYRENNE: Oh – cavalry. I didn't see him much. I spent my time painting and writing. I wrote a book when I was fourteen. Thirty chapters. When I was twelve I – *(she stops)* something else happened. *(She rises suddenly.)* I think I'll wear my jewellery. Just for you, Percy. Let's dress up. *(She picks up the tray and hurries towards the kitchen.)*

PERCY: I'd have worn me medals if I'd known. *(He laughs.)*

CYRENNE: How d'you mean? *(She pauses in the kitchen opening, seeming strangely tense.)* What did you mean by that?

PERCY: *(Surprised.)* It was a joke – just a joke.

CYRENNE: Oh. *(She laughs uncertainly.)* Would you find my jewel box in the tallboy, please? *(She goes into the kitchen and puts the tray on the dresser.)*

PERCY: Certainly. *(He goes to the tallboy up R.)*

CYRENNE: *(Calling.)* Oh, it may be the second drawer.

PERCY: What sort of box?

CYRENNE: A little white one.

(PERCY opens the second drawer and closes it again, standing away from it. CYRENNE returns from the kitchen, opens the drawer

and finds her jewel box. PERCY doesn't quite know where to look. Watching him levelly, CYRENNE closes the drawer very slowly.)

Don't say you're that green!

PERCY: I'm a bachelor, you know.

CYRENNE: Yes. Now then. *(She sorts through the box.)* Yes, let's have this one. *(Placing the box on the tallboy, she hands him a cheap chain medallion; then turns her back for him to fasten it on.)* I used to have lots of these but I sold them. Don't like memories. *(She turns round.)* Nice?

PERCY: Yes, it's all right.

CYRENNE: I feel like dancing. Can you?

PERCY: *(Irritably.)* Oh, yes. I used to run a dancing school.

CYRENNE: *(Laughing.)* Really?

PERCY: *(Shaking his head.)* I was joking. No, I wasn't even doing that. I was being sarcastic. Take no notice. *(He wanders c.)*

CYRENNE: Are you still embarrassed?

PERCY: Don't be soft. I've been around. No, it's the way you say things. It wasn't "Shall we dance" or "Let's dance", it was "Can you?"

CYRENNE: *(Sitting on the end of the bed.)* Not everybody can dance.

PERCY: Well, it so happens I can. You know, you make me feel as though I came up the Thames on a pogo stick ... Well, even if I did, it had a bell on – aw, forget it. I'm just grousing, I suppose. But each topic that crops up, you have a cupboardful: with your chauffeurs and white pillars, daffodils and Old Wob; brigadiers; money. You paint and you write. Thirty chapters at fourteen! Phew! I'm just about going under.

(CYRENNE mooches to the dressing-table, her hands behind her back.)

CYRENNE: It wasn't a very good book: terribly immature.

PERCY: Premature'd be a better word. Thirty chapters! Takes me half an hour to sign a Christmas card.

CYRENNE: *(Sitting on the stool.)* You do all this clever-research business.

PERCY: I only collate figures the Boffins have turned out. I collate them, you know. Oh, it's quite clever. I mean, I am clever at figures. But I don't suppose you'd want to spend the night adding figures together.

CYRENNE: *(Wickedly.)* Not on paper!

(PERCY says nothing to this, and she laughs.)

PERCY: I know what you mean. It's all right. There's another thing! I wouldn't dare say things to women at the mill that you say to me.

CYRENNE: You might have more fun if you did.

PERCY: I do very nicely, thank you. Oh, I realize it's very broadminded and Bohemian but ... not that I'm a prude. Don't get me wrong! I'm not a prude by a long chalk. I'm no angel. It's just that ... phew! Early on I felt really exhilarated. It was the meshing – yes, the meshing of our personalities. But suddenly my ego's – well, it's squashed; it's beat; worse than that, it's bu – well, I won't be rude.

CYRENNE: Go on! I dare you!

PERCY: You know what I mean.

CYRENNE: *(Agreeing.)* Mm. *(She sighs heavily, humorously.)*

(PERCY bites the edge of his thumb.)

PERCY: Oh – I'm no good with women. I'm like a chapel hatpeg. I'm everything the French laugh at in the English. *(He rises and follows a pattern on the carpet with his feet.)* I told you a lie when I said I had a particular girlfriend. I haven't. I know lots of girls – no, I don't! Lots know me, let's put it that way. I can't explain why

I've no steady girl. I'm old enough. Just never got round to it, I suppose. I'm kept pretty busy most of the time. Friday there's a get-together with the lads. You know.

CYRENNE: *(Nodding.)* The lads. *(She imitates his accent, but without irony: with kindly acceptance, if anything.)*

PERCY: Yes. Saturday's darts; Wednesday I spend with the Old Chilvington's Grammar School; Mondays I go to the pictures; and there's always television if the worst comes to the worst. The week goes by. I don't especially need anyone else.

CYRENNE: It's a problem, isn't it!

PERCY: No! That's what I'm explaining. I'm not moaning and whining, I'm just talking. Why don't you say something? I'm very well off on the quiet; nice bit in the bank; and I shall eventually go abroad for the firm. *(He fishes a squashed, empty cigarette packet out of his pocket.)* I shall have a secretary and a telephone.

CYRENNE: Take one of mine.

PERCY: No, thanks. I'm still full of feathers. *(He examines his face in the dressing-table mirror.)* Beginning to need a shave, too.

CYRENNE: *(Rising.)* There's only washing soap, but I can supply the rest. *(She takes a razor from her dressing-table.)* It is a new blade.

PERCY: *(Moving C.)* Who does it belong to?

CYRENNE: Me.

PERCY: Why should you have a – oh. Um. *(He backs hurriedly L.)* It's kind of you, but I think I'll wait till morning.

CYRENNE: Your whiskers! *(She replaces the razor.)*

PERCY: You don't want to watch me shaving.

CYRENNE: Yes, I do. I like it. It's manly.

PERCY: No, I prefer to wait, if you don't mind. I hate messing around in a shirt and collar. I like to strip off and get down to it.

CYRENNE: That's my boy! *(She smiles and crosses to LC with a saucy wink.)*

PERCY: *(Near to blushing.)* Oh, you're too sexy by far!

CYRENNE: Isn't it expected of me? *(She brings an ashtray from the table down L and empties it in the waste-paper basket R.)*

PERCY: You're not so tough as you make out! *(He grins.)* Mind you, there is a sort of X Certificate in the air – I'm just kidding! But it is a strange feeling being here. I mean me! Oh, you wouldn't understand.

CYRENNE: *(Bristling.)* Because I'm different?

PERCY: Well, yes, you must be. I mean, I shall have tonight's atmosphere with me for – oh, for – well, I'll tell you: the other week I saw a dog run over. Poor little dachshund, it was; just lay in the gutter, yelping and screeching; everyone stood round, hoping it'd die quickly. And the chap who owned it – must have been six foot four – beefy fella, he was crying like a baby. Apparently it was a very old dog he was taking to be put to sleep; but the poor little thing jumped right out of his arms under this truck. It was going to die anyhow – but to think it had to go like that! All its legs crushed. *(He shudders.)* I was cold inside for days. And yet tonight, after a fashion, I have the same kind of-pungency. Yes, that's the word. Pungency. But you wouldn't appreciate that.

CYRENNE: You think I have no feelings?

PERCY: Oh, yes, but our levels of sensitivity are ...

CYRENNE: *(Angrily.)* Strange as it seems, I'm sad when a little dog dies.

PERCY: Yes, maybe, but ...

CYRENNE: I have salt in my tears just like you.

PERCY: I know. I know...

CYRENNE: Then ram this past your halo, Percy. I'm no different to anyone else. I eat ordinary food, wear my best clothes in church, and never read dirty books at breakfast. Forget the dishes. Just blow!

PERCY: You don't half take offence!

CYRENNE: Here's the key of the door. *(She takes it from the bowl and lays it on the dressing-table.)* "The lads" are waiting!

PERCY: Did you have it all the time, then?

(CYRENNE covers her face with her hands.)

Are you crying?

(CYRENNE shakes her head and gives a short defiant laugh. From the dressing-table she takes a woolly toy dog and holds it close to her cheek, as though it is an old friend-when-in-need.)

I shouldn't want to leave you like this.

CYRENNE: Don't skin your nose! Everyone leaves me like this.

PERCY: I'll be happy to wash the pots, if you like.

CYRENNE: Some of them bluster, some of them swagger; but they mostly creep away.

PERCY: Or I'll attend to any odd jobs you may have outstanding. I'm in no hurry for an hour – if you have any squeaky floor-boards or faulty light switches or things that need oiling.

(CYRENNE does not answer.)

I promise not to break anything.

(CYRENNE laughs.)

CYRENNE: "He's good for me, Moma. He's awful good." That's a line from a book I once read. It was a book about a family in the Deep South, a family of rotters. All the Deep South families are rotters according to books and films. Have you noticed? Anyway, this girl used to get up in the morning, in the steaming heat, and throw on a thin cotton dress and run into the forest.

PERCY: Was it a film?

CYRENNE: Don't know; but she didn't wash or anything: and she never wore knickers. I used to think it was terribly saucy, this teenage belle among all these sweaty men, guns, dogs – and no knickers. In one part she went swimming with a boy called Aaron; naturally they had no costumes either; and so she had a baby. Everyone hated Aaron because he wore boots or something; and when this baby came, the girl's brothers captured him in the forest.

PERCY: Yes, I think it was a film. I remember.

CYRENNE: And two of them held him down while the others kicked him in the stomach. I gave myself a headache crying. *(She rises.)* Do you wear boots, Percy?

PERCY: Only for football.

(CYRENNE laughs and moves up R, into the kitchen, turning on the light and taking an apron from the dresser.)

CYRENNE: And for hiking? Are you the type who camps out in summer?

PERCY: *(Following her into the kitchen.)* I have done in my time, yes.

CYRENNE: *(Handing him the apron.)* Mind your nice suit! Use the squeeze-in soap on the draining-board.

PERCY: Oh, lovely! Right you are, then!

(CYRENNE helps him tie the apron.)

CYRENNE: *(Thoughtfully.)* Are you a scoutmaster? .

PERCY: *(Guiltily.)* What – what would be wrong in that?

CYRENNE: Nothing. Use the towel you had before.

(The telephone rings. CYRENNE enters the bedroom and lies on the bed to answer it.)

(Into the receiver.) Yes? ... Hello, Willie-darling! ... All right; and you? *(She laughs intimately.)*

(PERCY, in the kitchen, listens jealously.)

... Well, you shouldn't run about with nothing on ... I did no such thing! ... Oh, no, it was your idea! *(To PERCY.)* Don't break anything, will you, love?

PERCY: No.

CYRENNE: *(Into the receiver.)* I wasn't talking to you, Willie ... Yes. Jealous? ... Mind your own business! ... *(She laughs.)* Go to a party tonight? ... What sort of party?

(PERCY pricks up his ears.)

... Yacht? What kind of yacht? ... I've never been to a party on a yacht ... Hang on!

(PERCY has been disappointed by the turn of the telephone conversation. Now CYRENNE masks the receiver with her hand.)

(To Percy.) Do you really want to stay awhile?

PERCY: I don't want to stop you having ...

CYRENNE: I asked you if you wanted to stay.

PERCY: Yes. But I mean ...

CYRENNE: Whatever happens?

PERCY: How d'you mean?

(CYRENNE smiles.)

CYRENNE: *(Into the receiver.)* No go, Willie! My boy-friend won't let me.

PERCY: No, wait a minute ... !

CYRENNE: Ssssh! *(Into the receiver.)* What did you say? ... Oh, he's just a fella who does the washing up. G'-bye. *(She replaces the receiver.)*

PERCY: Well! It's very nice of you.

(CYRENNE rolls off the L side oj the bed and picks up a tiny transistor radio Jrom the bedside table.)

CYRENNE: It was only a friend of mine who has a motor-boat in Maidenhead.

PERCY: It might have been fun.

CYRENNE: I've been on the Queen Mary. Come on! Let's dance! Is that the correct phrase?

PERCY: Well. ... there's all those dishes, you know.

CYRENNE: God! D'you call that entertainment? *(She moves C.)* Come on, Man! I'm waiting. *(By now she has switched on the radio, which is blaring gay music – loud and swingy.)*

(PERCY enters from the kitchen, moves to her and tentative?; takes her arms. He breaks away immediately.)

PERCY: It's no use. I can't. When the lads go dancing I stay in the bar.

CYRENNE: Well, I'm damned! *(She clicks off the radio and tosses it on the bed.)* We have one hell of a scene because I say something wrong ... !

PERCY: Yes, well, all right, I know! So I told a lie. I just wanted to be able to say I could do something – that's why.

(CYRENNE crosses to the dressing-table and smoothes her eyebrows at the mirror.)

CYRENNE: I sacrificed champagne and oysters for you, love.

PERCY: Nobody twisted your arm. Why did you, anyway?

CYRENNE: Because I have clicking in the ears. I must have! Do you play tiddly-winks?

PERCY: No, I don't play tiddly-winks.

CYRENNE: You play darts, though.

PERCY: Yes. Why, have you got a board?

CYRENNE: Oh, no!

PERCY: More funny stuff. Very droll.

(CYRENNE flops face down on to the bed. She feels the radio, and switches it on. Then she eases off the bed, carrying the radio, and sidles to PERCY at LC, twisting her body in time to the music.)

CYRENNE: Well, Percival – *(She stands very close to him, her "motors" still running.)* what are we going to do?

PERCY: Well-as I said before, those dishes don't get any cleaner.

(He backs away to R and hurries into the kitchen.)

CYRENNE shrugs, turns up the radio, and dances with a cheval mirror as her partner. She whirls round and around, admiring herself. The mirror (catching the stage-electrics) reflects 'lightning' bursts out-and-across the auditorium. PERCY steals glances, easing from the Kitchen, dishcloth in hand. CYRENNE circles him dancing, bumping him, until PERCY takes the big decision and throws aside his dishcloth.

PERCY: Alright, alright! I can offer you an old-fashioned waltz – if I must.

CYRENNE: Why Percival – *(replacing the mirror)* – how gallant!

PERCY: Nowt fancy. And no clever comments.

PERCY grits his teeth, shuffling into action with the grace of a reluctant camel. Inevitably he takes a wrong step –

CYRENNE: Damn and blast!

– painfully, CYRENNE limps to sit on the bed-end. She removes her slipper; rubs her foot.

PERCY: Sorry.

CYRENNE: You have feet like a Yeti!

PERCY: Sorry.

CYRENNE: I'm crippled.

PERCY: Sorry.

(The record ends and a foreign announcer jabbers away. PERCY laughs.)

What's he saying?

CYRENNE: How should I know? Switch it off.

PERCY: *(Switching it off.)* 1 thought you spoke three languages.

CYRENNE: Only the swear words.

PERCY: It sounded like French.

CYRENNE: *(Replacing her slipper.)* Come and talk to me.

PERCY: All right. *(He moves down and stands R of her.)*

CYRENNE: Yes?

PERCY: Yes what?

CYRENNE: Yes what? Where are your manners? "Yes pardon!"

(She tugs his arm.)

(PERCY sits R of her on the bed.)

Go on, then! Start!

PERCY: Start what?

CYRENNE: Talking.

PERCY: You can't just start talking!

CYRENNE: Try! Say "I run a cotton factory" ...

PERCY: I don't. I just work there.

CYRENNE: By yourself, or are there lots of people?

PERCY: Only about three thousand!

CYRENNE: All men?

PERCY: Phew! No! Only a third are men.

CYRENNE: There! We've started talking. Now, we have – oh, I can't add – say a thousand available women, at least. So, every day at the factory you rampage among a thousand juicy women.

41

PERCY: What's all this rampaging?

CYRENNE: Why not?

PERCY: I'm stuck in the lab most of the time.

CYRENNE: You stop for lunch.

PERCY: People don't rampage in the canteen! D'you think we have some kind of orgy during lunch break?

CYRENNE: Lovely! *(She slides from the bed to the floor.)*

PERCY: Anyway, what're you driving at? I may not be going steady but I've taken girls out on dates. I've taken out plenty of girls.

CYRENNE: You've never slept with one.

(PERCY is shocked. He gets to his feet.)

PERCY: Phew! I reckon you'd walk into Marks and Spencer's and shout Woolworth's! You don't know what I've done.

CYRENNE: Don't you think it's time you did?

PERCY: Who says I haven't?

(CYRENNE smiles and shrugs.)

(Capitulating.) All right I haven't! I never have. *(He crosses below her to L.)* So you can laugh; laugh as much as you like.

CYRENNE: I'm not laughing.

PERCY: No, well ... ! *(He runs his fingers along the back of the armchair LC.)* I've had plenty of chances but I've never-followed them through. I don't have the technique, so Bob's your uncle. May I have one of your cigarettes now?

CYRENNE: 'Course.

(PERCY moves to the dressing-table and takes a cigarette from her packet.)

PERCY: I live with the family, you see. I must get somewhere on my own. Time I did. You can't take friends back home, really. There's only the spare parlour; and even if I did, Mother'd make it a ceremony – fussing, bringing out the posh spoons, dressing up. I'm not grousing – me mother's a wonderful woman. Wonderful. But I once took home a girl called Cherry; just a friend, nothing more. But what a palaver! There's me mother twittering away, nudging me father – little sidelong looks at each other. I froze up. You see, you don't know if you want the posh spoons until – *(He lights his cigarette.)* Anyway, I froze up.

CYRENNE: And Cherry?

PERCY: *(Grinning.)* She crystallized! I didn't see her for dust.

CYRENNE: And all these other dates?

PERCY: *(Sitting R of her on the floor.)* Well, if you've any advice it's most welcome, Cyrenne. Everything goes fine, you see, until near the end; then it's always the same – always the same long agonizing walk back to their gate. Truly agonizing, believe me! Talk about a dumb-bell – it has blood compared to me! I worry about this goodnight kissing business all the way to the gate.

CYRENNE: Can't that wait till the next night?

PERCY: I'm afraid not. I never get a return match. No, it's the good-night kissing business. Mind you, I've done plenty of ordinary kissing; at parties and – well, just at parties, I suppose. But when I reach the gate and she says "Thanks for a nice evening", or some such phrase, and I know she's expecting – expecting me to get romantic; and – aw, the whole thing goes to pot.

CYRENNE: A lot of men find ... *(She changes her mind.)* Why don't you let yourself go for once?

PERCY: Aye, I did try for once! The girl laughed; and she said – *(He stops.)*

CYRENNE: Said what?

PERCY: *(Obviously deeply hurt by this at the time.)* – she said, "You'd better stick to training Boy Scouts, Percy." *(Defensively.)* Yes, you guessed right. I am a scoutmaster. And I'm fed up feeling embarrassed when I tell people. Oh, life's a mess, it really is!

(There is a slight pause.)

CYRENNE: It'll sort itself out and ...

PERCY: Anyway, I even asked Ginger. He's a smooth type, you know. He has one dance with a girl then disappears with her. Half an hour later he comes back looking smug and satisfied. So I asked him straight out. I said, "What d'you say to a woman when you've got her to yourself?" "Come on," he said, "I'll show you." He stopped the first girl he met in the corridor, and started making love to her!

CYRENNE: In the corridor?

PERCY: The neck of the man! Fantastic! Fantastic! Even with me there he went so far as to tell her ... still, I'll not repeat it.

CYRENNE: Why, was it rude?

PERCY: Not really, but I can't tell you.

CYRENNE: Oh, come on, tell me.

PERCY: *(Squirming.)* "Well – ", he said – "What – what beautiful breasts you have." Now I feel a chump for telling you. *(Thoroughly embarrassed, he jumps to his feet and moves up R, then across to L.)* There's nothing in it, I realize that. Everyone's broad-minded today. They talk openly about things my grandmother would've fainted at.

CYRENNE: Look – *(She sighs.)* Percy, didn't your grandma have breasts?

PERCY: Well – eh?

CYRENNE: I know mine did. I remember she had a gigantic bust which entered a room several seconds before she did. She was proud of it. She was French – a marchioness – terribly old family. You're not old-fashioned, love – you're unbelievable.

PERCY: Well, I think my grandmother would've fainted.

CYRENNE: God help your grandpa's honeymoon!

PERCY: All right, pull my leg!

CYRENNE: Is this what Ginger meant by "Remember the top half"?

PERCY: When did he say that?

CYRENNE: He yelled it several times before he fell off the taxi.

PERCY: That's Ginger all over.

CYRENNE: But not you anywhere. A shame! *(She rises, pops her head over his shoulder and asks huskily.)* Shall I order one pint of milk tomorrow, or two?

PERCY: Milk?

CYRENNE: *(With a humorous sigh.)* I'm afraid one'll be enough.

> *(PERCY sits in the chair L. He removes the rattle from under him and places it on the table. CYRENNE goes into the kitchen for an empty milk bottle.)*

PERCY: I'm not so pure as all that. I'm average.

CYRENNE: Stretching it a bit at thirty-five, don't you think? *(She crosses from the kitchen to the door up L, goes out, opens the front door, and puts out the milk bottle.)*

PERCY: *(Strongly.)* No, I don't. The people you meet aren't a true cross-section; not representative. I believe there're many folks like me who haven't the facets – yes, the facets. They haven't the facets to make friends easily. That doesn't mean they're warped or retarded, you know. There's nothing wrong with them. If anything...

CYRENNE: *(Closing the door up L and moving to C.)* Yes, I know! It's all my fault.

PERCY: Well, I don't go around doing peculiar things, you know; or writing on walls. *(He starts to laugh.)*

CYRENNE: Now what?

PERCY: Oh, it's um – it's nothing.

CYRENNE: Percy, only nut-cases laugh at nothing; and it's terribly bad-mannered.

PERCY: I was, um – I was thinking about the mill canteen; and on one of the doors in the – well, in the Gentlemen's Room, d'you see – someone has written "A Happy New Year To all Our Readers"! *(He goes into ecstacies of merriment.)* I think that's very funny, don't you?

CYRENNE: *(Dryly.)* You must remember to tell Ginger.

PERCY: Yes. *(He laughs again.)* No. It was Ginger told me. Oh, I'm sorry. It was rude.

(CYRENNE smiles and kneels by his side.)

CYRENNE: You're very sweet, Percival – quite normal – and quite, quite untouchable. *(Suddenly, as though unable to keep her hands away from him, she scrubs at his chest and makes a loud comic growling sound. Then she rises and moves to C, stretching luxuriously.)* Oooogh! Now I wish I'd gone to the yacht party. All at once I'm in the mood for wine, men and song.

PERCY: Oh, I'm batting at zero, boring you in the bargain.

CYRENNE: Don't worry, my pet. Some woman'll materialize and your stuttering lips'll blossom into poetry. Where are those blasted tissues? *(She looks around the room.)* She'll listen enraptured to your Lancashire sweet nothings. She'll come – and she won't laugh.

PERCY: She's taking a heck of a long time.

CYRENNE: At thirty-five! No, no! Beautiful age; everyone says so; beautiful! *(She goes into the kitchen.)* Oh, she'll come from somewhere, sometime; maybe tomorrow; and you'll be in clover. *(She laughs.)* I haven't thought as you do since I was twelve. I painted a picture of a naked boy when I was twelve. *(She switches off the kitchen light and comes back into the room.)*

PERCY: I dare say we all ...

CYRENNE: *(Crossing to the tallboy.)* From a model, love. I made him strip off and stand by an old water butt in the yard. He was – he lived in the same street. *(She laughs and opens a tallboy drawer, taking out the missing tissues; then she wipes her nose, throws the tissue into a waste-paper basket, and takes the box to the dressing-table.)* Anyway, it rained and he caught a chill. Then I took the painting to school and caused a scandal – it was a riot in fact! You should have seen the teachers! Oh, it was delicious! They sent me home, called my parents. Reporters came – big splash in the local rag – altogether it was a bloody good do.

PERCY: Did you say "parents"?

CYRENNE: S-Stepmother. Father married again.

PERCY: You said you painted him by a water butt in a yard. A boy from the same street.

CYRENNE: That's right.

PERCY: I thought you lived in a big house.

CYRENNE: *(Hesitating.)* I was staying with an aunt. She wasn't so well-off.

PERCY: I see.

CYRENNE: So, that was when I was twelve. By the time I reached sixteen I was really whooping it up.

PERCY: You must have had quite a life.

CYRENNE: Yes, sirree! *(She crosses to behind his chair.)* Just fancy, though! Sweet thirty-five and still full of excitement and naughty thoughts. Never mind, pet. You're on top. *(Sadly, and full of yearning.)* I can't even remember a first dance or a first kiss. Think I've been kissing and dancing since – God knows – since Adam.

PERCY: You're not so tremendously old.

CYRENNE: My story is twenty-four, Mr Winthram. A hundred and twenty-four, to you. I know! *(She moves to the side of his chair.)* My old paint-box is still handy. Shall I paint you – in the raw?

PERCY: Oh. *(He laughs.)* There's no-one I could show it to.

CYRENNE: I don't mean a picture. I mean paint you – all over.

(She tickles him energetically.)

(PERCY goes into fits of anguished laughter.)

We'd use blue because you'd be cold and shocked, green for your past, and orange dabs for the blushes yet to come. *(Again she tickles him.)*

(PERCY rocks with laughter and I beg her to cease.)

PERCY: Oh dear, oh dear, oh dear! *(He becomes suddenly serious.)*

Are you taking the mickey?

CYRENNE: *(Shaking her head and running a finger along his neck and round his ear.)* No. I'm envying your carbolic-scrubbed life. D'you have Scout mistresses?

PERCY: In a way. We call them Guide leaders.

CYRENNE: Lean your head over.

PERCY: Mm?

CYRENNE: Against me. *(She sits on the arm of his chair, draws his head to her breast, and soothes his brow with her hand.)* You're not missing much, love. Haven't you heard them say love is an overrated pastime? But-but if you really ... *(She pauses, then pushes him gently away and goes over to the bed.)* No, I mustn't steal. *(She sits on the end of the bed and reaches for her diary.)* It must have taken guts for you to come here tonight.

PERCY: *(Rising.)* Frankly, I don't remember much; so I can't claim guts. Besides I'm glad. I'm – I'm damn glad, and I'd like you to know that.

CYRENNE: Yes, you've told me. I'm honoured.

PERCY: I mean it.

CYRENNE: So do I. It's All Souls' Night. Everyone loves everyone - everyone wears wings. *(She opens her diary.)*

PERCY: Are you regretting missing the party?

CYRENNE: *(Looking up.)* I'm pondering the alternative arrangements. You know, a performance indoors if it rains. *(She smiles.)* But even the roof is leaking.

PERCY: Let's – let's get down to brass tacks. You're talking about making love to me, aren't you?

(CYRENNE nods and gently mimics his accent.)

CYRENNE: Brass tacks.

(On an impulse, PERCY goes and sits L of her.)

PERCY: I'd like to, Cyrenne. I-I'd like to. I'd like to kiss you... and hold you, and say things. Cyrenne, I want. . . . *(He makes a grab jor her hand and, in doing so, knocks her diary to the floor. He looks at the fallen book, then turns away.)* Oh, blast!

CYRENNE: *(Picking it up.)* Doesn't matter. I'm always kicking it around.

(But the moment has gone. PERCY intertwines his fingers and examines them.)

PERCY: Well, that's me: clumsy to the end! Bang on form!

CYRENNE: Never mind. *(Coaxing.)* Percy? – Percival?

PERCY: I don't. I'm used to it.

CYRENNE: Where else did you go tonight? Mm? Come on, love. Snap out of the gloom.

PERCY: Last thing I remember's Piccadilly Circus: dancing in a ring round Eros. Then a policeman moves us on. Oh, yes! We went to a club next. Wait a minute! *(He racks his brains.)* Yes! Phew!

Cigarettes ten bob! Ten bob for cigarettes! And Ginger! *(He laughs.)*

He was singing with the band. Next thing I remember's being thrown out. Then we went to your club and met you ... Hang on, though! Wait a minute! *(He rises, eyes wide.)* Oh, Jemima! Now I've got it! We had a bet.

CYRENNE: You and Ginger?

PERCY: Yes. *(He backs away to L.)* He bet me I wouldn't –

CYRENNE: – go home with me?

PERCY: Yes.

CYRENNE: How much?

PERCY: I've a dreadful feeling it was – *(he gulps.)* fifty pounds.

CYRENNE: Including expenses? *(She is enjoying this.)*

PERCY: *(Tragically.)* Streuth! I must've been bonkers.

CYRENNE: You should be pleased. I am. I didn't know I was worth so much.

PERCY: Don't joke about it, please!

CYRENNE: You've won, haven't you? You're here!

PERCY: No, I haven't won. That's the whole point. It wasn't merely a question of coming home. I was supposed to ... Anyway, I haven't won.

CYRENNE: O-oh! Well now! *(She writes in her diary.)*

PERCY: Cyrenne, seeing that ...

CYRENNE: It'll all be forgotten by tomorrow.

PERCY: It won't, you know! Borrow threepence from Ginger and he's waiting with his hand out next day. Very strong principles, has Ginger.

CYRENNE: *(Still writing.)* So you'll have to tell a fib after all.

PERCY: I couldn't now. No point in making a bet if you don't stick to the bargain. Oh, this is horrible. *(He paces in silence.)* This is horrible!

CYRENNE: *(Angrily.)* Look, if you find me so damned horrible, go lick your wounds somewhere else!

PERCY: I'm sorry: I didn't intend any ...

CYRENNE: Just phone a cab, Percy. It's late; I'm tired; and you're worried.

PERCY: *(Hotly.)* Oh, it's always me! *(He strides to the telephone up L.)*

CYRENNE: *(Quietly.)* There's a taxi number on the light switch.

(PERCY dials a number. CYRENNE reads aloud from her diary.)

"Saturday. Eleven-fifteen. Met Percy Winthram. Exclamation mark! Talked of life and disappointments. Felt someone looking over my shoulder for the first time in years. Exclamation mark!"

PERCY: Cyrenne ...

CYRENNE: Sssh! No.

PERCY: Oh, heck!

CYRENNE: "I wonder what will become of him; and if he'll think of me? Cue for song." *(She throws the diary behind her on to the bed; then rises and moves down L.)* Any luck?

PERCY: It's ringing.

CYRENNE: They'll answer. Let yourself out, love. And next time you date a girl, try forcing your luck.

(CYRENNE goes out down L. PERCY hangs up. He dials a fresh number, after consulting a card taken from his pocket.)

PERCY: *(Into the receiver.)* Hello? Is that the Pablo Private
Hotel, please? ... Oh. This is Mr Winthram. Has Mr
Grappley returned yet, please? ... Thank you. *(He waits
impatiently, saying to himself.)* I'm fighting time now; and
I'm too damn scared to wind the clock. Oh, what if he's
not back? What if he's plastered down some alley? *(Into
the receiver.)* Hello, Ginger? It's Perce ... Perce! ...Fine.
I got on fine ... I er, came home with her, yes ... Yes ...
Talking ... It's all so far, yes ... Ginge, listen! Don't you
think it's a bit stupid all this? ... I'm not backing out at all.
Frankly, I'm giving you a chance. I mean, I'm here. I'm
here, Ginge. Just a matter of time, that's all ... Hello? ...
D'you still want to go through with it, then? . . . Who's
dead scared. Ha! . . . Hello? . . . Hello? ... Ginger? ... *(He
hangs up gloomily.)* Fool! Stupid fool! Throwing his money
around! Fifty pounds on a damn stupid bet.

*PERCY staggers tragically to the bed-end; sits; then slides to the
floor, groaning.*

PERCY: Ee, why wasn't I born a rabbit!

CURTAIN

ACT TWO

PERCY is slumped at the bed-end, snoring.

CYRENNE ENTERS DL. She is wearing a stylish electric-blue cocktail dress – and in herself seems cooler, more the duchess than coquette. She nudges PERCY with her toe:

CYRENNE: Percy! Your Mother wants you.

PERCY: Aw, not Monday again. It's always Monday.

CYRENNE: And Ginger is waiting – *(growls.)* – for his gold.

PERCY: *(Scrambles to his feet.)* Oh 'eck! You churned me mind's giblets. It's so demeaning - being caught dozing.

CYRENNE: Percy, love, you get complicateder and complicateder. Zip me up, there's a sweet.

PERCY: Are you off somewhere?

CYRENNE: Going back to the club.

PERCY: *(Struggling with the zip.)* Phew! It's an awkward zip.

CYRENNE: Only going up ... Well done! *(She moves to her tallboy; and we see that her dress is ninety per cent backless, with a tiny ten per cent zip. She opens her jewellery box and extracts a bracelet.)*

PERCY: I rang up Ginger.

CYRENNE: Did you?

PERCY: Yes. Oh, I owe you fourpence. *(Moving to the bedside table, he gets out four pennies and puts them down on it.)*

CYRENNE: *(Holding out her arm across the bed.)* More help, please.

PERCY: *(Putting on the bracelet.)* Don't you want to hear what he said?

CYRENNE: If you like.

PERCY: He wouldn't give up the bet.

CYRENNE: You know Ginger! Thank you. *(She crosses to the dressing-table and dabs perfume on her wrists.)*

PERCY: Shall you be seeing anyone special?

CYRENNE: Probably.

PERCY: You look nice.

CYRENNE: Do I?

PERCY: Oh, what's the matter? Everything's gone – I don't know. Is it because I said "horrible"?

CYRENNE: No, that's forgotten.

PERCY: If you're cheesed because I messed up your evening. I'm sorry. Honestly. I'm so clumsy, so flipping clumsy.

CYRENNE: No, you're not.

PERCY: Then why have you gone so cold?

(CYRENNE take his hand, smiles at him sadly. Then the moment passes.)

CYRENNE: But we don't really mix now, do we! Not really. So you're going to Euston and I'm going to see where they buried Saint Pancras.

(CYRENNE pats his hand and releases it.)

PERCY: Cy-Cyrenne, I had butterflies all yesterday thinking of the trip down here. I kept remembering: "It's a holiday tomorrow. A holiday!" So why shouldn't I make it one? If – if you'll be as you were before. If you'll be warm: you know – warm – I think this time I could ...

(The doorbell rings. They both turn. PERCY slaps his fist in plaintive frustration.)

PERCY: Oh, why did it have to ring now! *(Urgently.)* I mustn't – I can't miss my chance. If you'd only be friendly again...

(The doorbell rings. CYRENNE moves to the dressing-table and picks up the door-key.)

CYRENNE: Well, once you get in the fresh air ...

(Again the doorbell. She hands the key to Percy, crossing him to down L.)

Open up, love, before they break in.

(CYRENNE exits down L.)

PERCY: Ee, I wish I were different. *(He unlocks and opens the door, then moves into the corridor. He opens the front door.)*

(RICARD enters. He is a handsome Latin type in his late twenties. Perhaps there is a trace of weakness in his face. He is changeable – excitable – very much like CYRENNE, in fact. He ignores PERCY and moves into the room. He crosses immediately to the kitchen, taking in his surroundings en route.)

PERCY: I'm er, pleased to meet you.

(RICARD peers into the kitchen, then calls.)

RICARD: Cinny! Cinny!

(CYRENNE hurries in down L.)

CYRENNE: Ricky! Ricky-love! *(She runs to him.)* What a surprise.

RICARD: *(To PERCY.)* Would you mind? This is personal.

PERCY: Oh, er ...

RICARD: These yours? *(Without waiting for an answer, he takes PERCY's clothes from the banisters R and throws them across at him.)*

PERCY: Hey! Just a moment ... !

CYRENNE: *(Crossing to PERCY up L.)* Friend of the family, Percy. Excuse his bad manners.

PERCY: Is this how it ends, then?

CYRENNE: *(Indifferently.)* 'Fraid so, sweetie. Good luck with Ginger.

PERCY: Night-night. *(To RICARD.)* Night-night.

(PERCY makes a lonely exit. CYRENNE turns to face RICARD.)

CYRENNE: Any time you're passing, just pop in and kick out my friends.

RICARD: Friend, was he!

CYRENNE: That's right – friend. *(She laughs lightly.)* You know, this is fantastic. You stroll in after all this time, don't even toot your horn, just stroll in. *(She moves to him.)* How've you been, Ricky?

RICARD: *(Turning away slightly.)* Fine. You?

CYRENNE: *(Merrily.)* Things have happened; time's gone...

RICARD: *(Interrupting impatiently.)* I've come from moma and dad, Sis. Said I'd take you back tonight.

CYRENNE: Oh?

RICARD: They want to see you. They're opening a new restaurant. We're all going in – whole family. Me, Margo – and we need you as well.

CYRENNE: I've given up slaving in cafes, Ricky. No, thanks.

RICARD: *(In the same dull, stubborn tone.)* You can be manager; then we shan't have to go outside the family.

CYRENNE: Dad can manage it. You don't need me.

RICARD: I just promised you'd go back and talk to them.

CYRENNE: Ah! We're not talking very much these days, the family and me.

RICARD: Dad was very eager to have you...

CYRENNE: *(Strongly.)* He's not my father.

RICARD: All right, stepfather then. Where's your coat? I'm taking you back, Sis. *(He looks round the room, then crosses to the hooks up L.)*

CYRENNE: Just like that! Marvellous!

RICARD: You need only stop an hour; then I've done my bit. *(Unhooking her coat.)* This the one?

CYRENNE: Are they all there? Auntie Bo, Uncle Arturo, everyone?

RICARD: *(Moving to her.)* Aunt Bo's baby-sitting for Margo and me.

CYRENNE: Spaghetti's out, Ricky – got that? And I'm not attending any cookhouse conventions at this hour.

RICARD: No? What were your plans for tonight, Sis?

CYRENNE: *(Looking at him for a moment, then turning away up L.)* I spent my childhood in our old cafe and the very mention of cooking and cafes makes me ill.

RICARD: Well, anyway – tell them. *(He moves to her, holding up the coat.)*

CYRENNE: No. I said no!

RICARD: Come on!

(RICARD pulls her arm with the intention of helping her into her coat, but she pushes him away. A struggle develops between them, half brother-sister fight and half serious. It ends violently. They fall across the bed and CYRENNE strikes at his face and frees herself; then she rises and backs away, panting.)

RICARD: *(Clutching his cheek.)* You little bitch!

CYRENNE: So I'm not going anywhere tonight *(She re-hangs her coat behind the door.)* not anywhere.

RICARD: *(Rising.)* Not even on the prowl, Sis? On the beat?

(CYRENNE swings round, shocked.)

I know, Sis. I've seen you. Hadn't been off the ship a day! First person I met was old Tosky and he said, "I've seen your sister picking up men in a drinking club." I thanked him with a belt in the jaw. I was insulted. *(He laughs shortly.)* So to prove he was lying, I watched

57

outside that club of yours. I've watched for the last few days.

CYRENNE: That's a decent brotherly gesture.

RICARD: Were you decent, bringing men home? Two men, one after another! I was sick, physically sick. *(Cruelly.)* Been out tonight, have you?

CYRENNE: *(Almost hissing.)* Yes.

RICARD: *(Shouting.)* Fine! Good! I'm glad! Holy Mother, why d'you do it? Why did you start?

CYRENNE: *(Shaking her head dully.)* It's like I said: things've happened.

RICARD: My own sister – a prostitute.

(CYRENNE turns on him. Her voice is low, fierce, quivering with emotion.)

CYRENNE: Now listen, Ricky: you come into my house – this is my house – and you don't even ask how I am. You b-be good to me, Ricky.

RICARD: Oh, yes. I've every reason, of course. *(He picks a newspaper off the tallboy and toys with it.)*

CYRENNE: Well, you're not so clever! You go abroad for months on end leaving a wife and two kids.

RICARD: *(Moving C.)* I went on a job; and I've made money... good, clean, money.

CYRENNE: *(Shouting.)* Don't say "clean" to me! You don't know Ricky. You don't know. *(She moves behind the chair L.)* But since you're so damned sanctimonious, I'll tell you. Yes, why not! It was him, Ricky. He barged into my room and-and I was dressing.

RICARD: Who barged in?

CYRENNE: Moma took his side, as usual, but I'd done nothing...

RICARD: Who barged in?

CYRENNE: Dad. He was always like that with me. In the old cafe – that tiny kitchen – when he used to squeeze past me. And even upstairs.

RICARD: You're making it up. You're making it up to excuse yourself.

CYRENNE: *(Moving to him at c.)* No, Ricky: it was popa ...

RICARD: Stop it, Sis! You're lying again.

CYRENNE: I never lied to you, Ricky. Honest! Never to you.

RICARD: Will you button up!

(He moves away, shaking his hands at his ears, then comes back.):

What're you fighting, Sis? Why don't you come back? What's so peachy down-dingy-steps in this – this –

(RICARD swings around, gesticulating, his arms dismissive of CYRENNE's 'basement world'.).

– aw, come back, Sis. Momma's new Cafe's a Wow. It's snazzy, real snazzy. Proper restaurant. Murals. Guitarist at weekends.

CYRENNE: And what does Momma want me for? Bottle-washing?

RICARD: Aw, Sis – ! They were all there tonight, talking about you; saying how wonderful if Cinny came back. And Uncle Arturo – well, you know how excited he gets-said, "Let's pay a visit. Let's-a pay da visita pronto," he said. So I said I'd come. I saw them all arriving here and finding you – with someone, perhaps. It would have killed moma.

CYRENNE: *(Tonelessly.)* Oh, yes. Yes, it would.

RICARD: I haven't told them, you know; not even Margo.

CYRENNE: *(Lightly.)* Good. Thank you.

RICARD: Cinny, come and stay at Moma's tonight, eh? Just for me. Well – well, hell! We were always fighting or crying together always pretty damn close. Eh, Cinny?

CYRENNE: I can't. *(She shakes her head.)* I can't.

RICARD: I'm sorry about – about the way things are – Sorry.

CYRENNE: I wanted to marry you when I was young. I used to tell people: "I'm going to marry Ricky when I grow up."

RICARD: Remember when you almost hacked off my wrist making us blood brothers?

CYRENNE *(Shrugging.)* I happened to catch a vein.

RICARD: Yeah. *(He examines his wrist.)*

CYRENNE: I thought it'd hurt less if I used a blunt edge. It was the thing for taking Boy Scouts out of horses' hooves.

RICARD: Remember when you painted that picture of me and took it to school?

CYRENNE: Oh – that. I got a hell of a lecture from moma about brothers and sisters: what they were allowed to do and what they were not allowed to do.

RICARD: Moma?

CYRENNE: *(Nodding.)* She was quite different with me after that. She never took her eyes off me. Moma had me in the old cafe every possible minute-washing up, scraping leavings into that filthy tea-chest in the yard. Do you remember the steam beetles on the oven wall?

RICARD: No.

CYRENNE: I do. Once I dropped my cloth behind the stove pipe and when I pulled out my hand it was covered in steam beetles.

(She shudders.) It was my punishment, you see, Ricky.

(RICARD starts an impatient denial but she interrupts, nodding gravely.)

You know what she thought, what everyone thought! Oh, yes. Moma made herself very clear – even at my age.

(RICARD swings off the bed to L. He speaks strongly – almost violently, and one wonders if he is protesting to hide a conscience.)

RICARD: So I undressed while my own sister painted my picture: so what! I was only – I wasn't fourteen. I've led an ordinary, normal, healthy life. I've married; I have kids; Margo has no complaints. Anyway, it's past – forgotten. I don't know why I'm yapping.

CYRENNE: It started to rain and you wanted to go in; but I wouldn't let you. *(Rising, to meet him below c.)* So you ran and tattled to moma. You were always a tell-tale, Ricky. Used to like seeing me punished, didn't you, boy!

RICARD: Are you saying this is how it all started?

CYRENNE: Perhaps.

RICARD: Bringing me into it?

CYRENNE: "Perhaps" to that as well.

RICARD: *(Crossing her to R.)* Oh, great! Now it's my fault!

CYRENNE: I said "perhaps". *(Angrily.)* But it might help if you remembered it next time you call, instead of worrying about how you feel – how the family feels – how everyone feels except me! Oh, what the hell! I know you mean well, love. *(Impulsively she kisses him.)* I know you mean well. Want a drink?

RICARD: *(Nodding.)* Like I'm buried in sand!

CYRENNE: You bring the bottle, I'll fetch the glasses.

(CYRENNE goes into the kitchen, switching on the light, and collecting the tumblers from the dresser. RICARD moves to the tallboy for the whisky.)

Oh, I've got some stamps for little Ricky and Perry.

RICARD: Oh good, thanks. *(He uncorks the whisky and puts it on the dressing-table.)*

CYRENNE: One of the g – a girl friend gave them me. I'd told her I had two nephews.

RICARD: Thanks.

CYRENNE: Margo at the cafe? *(She switches off the light, returns to the bedroom with the glasses and pours two tots.)*

RICARD: Yes. Lunch-times ... Thanks, that's plenty. *(He moves away to C with his glass.)*

CYRENNE: Chow!

RICARD: Chow!

(They drink. CYRENNE puts down her glass on the dressing-table and hunts through various pots and boxes on her dressing-table-in search for the foreign stamps. Then she pauses, speaking to him over her shoulder.)

CYRENNE: Supposing-supposing I tried, Ricky?-No more lies and putting on airs; just plain, respectable me.

RICARD: Would you, Sis?

CYRENNE: Not spaghetti again: I couldn't try that saintly hard. Go in an office, maybe: nine till five and tennis afterwards. *(She faces him.)* That make you happy?

RICARD: 'Course it would.

CYRENNE: All right then, it's a deal. *(She spits on her hand and holds it out.)* Moko Poko!

RICARD: Poko magee!

(He spits on his hand, they clap twice, then shake. It is obviously some secret childhood ritual. She holds his hand for a second then quickly turns away and continues searching.)

CYRENNE: Where are those stamps? Tell you what! I'll bring them round tomorrow.

RICARD: *(Putting his glass on the dressing-table.)* To my place?

CYRENNE: Yes. I haven't seen your kids in ages.

RICARD: *(Uneasily.)* It's a bit difficult tomorrow, Sis. *(He moves C and sits on the pouffe.)*

CYRENNE: Monday then. *(Rummaging.)* Where are they!

RICARD: Trouble is Margo isn't ...

CYRENNE: Here they are! I'll make a huge parcel with these in the centre. *(She sorts through them.)*

RICARD: Don't go to any bother. Shall I take them?

CYRENNE: No, I want to see their faces.

RICARD: Only – you know Margo. She likes them in bed early and they're at school during the day.

CYRENNE: Any time suits me.

RICARD: It's only that um – the next few days – um, let's see now.

(He avoids looking in her direction.)

(CYRENNE is getting the message. She turns slowly and looks at him.)

CYRENNE: *(Evenly and deliberately.)* How about next Friday at six?

RICARD: Margo's folks are coming, I think.

CYRENNE: Saturday?

RICARD: Well – I'll think about it, eh?

(CYRENNE holds a hand to her mouth, tightly closing her eyes. She moves up R, a tremble in her voice:)

CYRENNE: What am I s-saying! *(She forces a laugh.)* I'm – I'm going away next week.

RICARD: You are?

CYRENNE: Switzerland. Winter sports. Yes. I've a boy-friend. Percival.

(She collects her glass from the dressing-table.) He's just dying to take me on holiday. All above-board – no hanky-panky with Percy. He was here when you arrived.

RICARD: *(Rising.)* Well, this is wonderful, Sis. Marvellous.

CYRENNE: Yes. *(She sits at her dressing-table.)* He's not a bad fellow; wants to marry me; always popping the question. He knows all about me.

RICARD: Well, what do you know! Cinny, why not? Eh? *(He claps his hands gaily.)* And I'll be best man.

CYRENNE: Mm.

RICARD: *(Heartily.)* You know, I've just thought-Friday would've been fine. Margo's folks aren't coming until. ...

CYRENNE: Don't push it, Ricky! *(In a whisper.)* I got the message. *(She drains her glass.)* Buzz off now, love.

(RICARD moves up for his coat, then comes down behind her.)

RICARD: This on the level, this holiday?

CYRENNE: Switzerland. Yes.

RICARD: Honest? I mean, all above-board and...

CYRENNE: I've had all I can take, Ricky.

RICARD: It's a fair question if you really mean to change.

(CYRENNE feels humiliated.)

CYRENNE: *(In a quiet, dead* voice: *)* I'll keep myself clean-wash my hands and nails. I'll send you a doctor's report.

RICARD: Aw, cut the music, Sis! I'm only asking for your word – your word of honour, that this Percy fella is ...

CYRENNE: *(Rebelling against this, and shouting.)* No! It's a lie. He's a nasty sordid gentleman who calls every Saturday. And I'll be in next Saturday when he calls – and the next after that.

RICARD: *(Yelling in return.)* And what about us? What when someone else says he's seen my sister? I can't break everybody's head.

CYRENNE: *(Rising.)* Try praying for me!

RICARD: It's a bit bloody late for that now.

(CYRENNE pushes past him to L. He tries to catch her arm, but she shakes him away.)

CYRENNE: Leave me alone, Ricky.

RICARD: All I'm asking is your word that...

CYRENNE: Will you leave me alone! Just leave me alone, will you?

(She is mentally beaten. She gives in and sobs, resting against the wall L and saying repeatedly.) Ricky, leave me alone ...

(RICARD exits up L. CYRENNE hears the door slam, and turns. On the table down L she sees PERCY's rattle. She moves to it, fondles it for a second or so, then drops it into the chair. She moves to the bed, flops down, and hugs her toy dog.)

I don't need them. I don't need anyone.

(The telephone rings. Eagerly she clutches the receiver to her ear.)

Yes? ... Yes ... Willie-darling, hello! ... Starting out for where? ...

No, thanks, love. I've been on the Queen Mary. *(Urgently.)* Come round here instead... Please, Willie. Please. Come and see me, Willie. Please come over... You'll be seasick! ...Yes. *(Dully.)* Some other time. *(She hangs up and wanders to the dressing-table. There she sits on her stool.)*

(The doorbell rings.)

(Calling.) It's not locked. *(She hurriedly repairs her make-up.)*

(PERCY enters up L.)

PERCY: I forgot my rattle.

(CYRENNE tries to laugh; but tears flow instead. She weeps silently.)

It isn't half cold, I've been round the block six times. No, seven. A policeman followed me last time round. Can I come in and get it? My rattle?

(CYRENNE nods her head. PERCY closes the door and moves down to above the armchair L.)

It isn't half cold. I saw two of the lads from our charabanc. Phew! Talk about sloshed! Their eyeballs were bottle shaped. I bet that copper's nabbed 'em by now. Hey, what's the matter?

CYRENNE: Nerves, I think.

PERCY: *(Crossing to her.)* Was it that chap?

CYRENNE: *(Shaking her head.)* It was my brother.

PERCY: Your brother? Oh, yes, he's the doctor. Oh, no – your brother runs the country club.

CYRENNE: He works in a cafe. It's my – it's a restaurant.

PERCY: We-ell, country club sounds better. We all put on airs, you know.

CYRENNE: Not you, Percy! You don't.

PERCY: Everyone. Our old man at the mill can hardly talk for the plums in his mouth; but nobody minds; he's a good enough boss. He's never afraid to admit he came from Wigan. There's a story going the rounds. Shall I tell you?

CYRENNE: Funny one?

PERCY: It's a tale – you know, a joke. I'm quite good at jokes. It might cheer you up.

CYRENNE: I doubt it – oh, I'm sorry – go on. Try.

PERCY: Well – *(He clears his throat.)* the managing director's wife called on the boss's wife, you see. Our boss's wife, I'm talking about. *(He shifts from foot to foot during this tale, delivering it as a party piece. He couldn't tell a joke to save his life.)* And the boss was in the garden; gardening. And he shouted out: "Ethel!" His wife's called Ethel. That's her name in real life. Anyway ... Wait a minute! Let me get it straight. Um – yes. The boss called out: "Ethel! Where's the manure for the roses?" It's not near the knuckle. *(He looks at her.)*

CYRENNE: Who said that?

PERCY: No, the joke isn't. It's a bit cheeky but – oh, I'll think of another.

CYRENNE: No. I like this one. I'm fascinated.

PERCY: Oh. Well, he shouted: "Ethel! Where's the manure for the roses?" and the managing director's wife said: "Oh, Ethel! Can't you make your husband say 'fertilizer'? It's much more refined." And the boss's wife said ... *(He giggles.)*

CYRENNE: Said what?

PERCY: "Make him say fertilizer! It's taken me ten years to make him say manure!" *(He roars with laughter.)*

(CYRENNE ponders the joke unenlightened. PERCY's laughter slowly fades as he notices her puzzlement.)

Don't you get it?

CYRENNE: I thought fertilizer and manure were the same thing.

PERCY: They are! But don't you see – he'd always called it ... ! Oh heck! I'm really up against the dots now. *(He scratches his head.)*

CYRENNE: Percy! It's only a piece of wood on a ratchet.

PERCY: Beg pardon?

CYRENNE: This rattle.

PERCY: *(Nodding.)* Yes, it was an excuse. *(He sits on the corner of the bed.)* D'you ever talk to yourself? I do. If I'm not feeling particularly sleepy at night, I go long walks round the town. And I talk to myself. Sometimes, if I haven't finished the conversation when I get back home, I go round again!

(CYRENNE smiles.)

Oh, I do! Anyway, tonight, round and round that block, I was talking to you. And this is what I said: if it's y-your

– d-desire to go with men; I mean, you as a woman do go ... *(He blurts out.)* You went cold with me. You lost interest. Surely I'm not so dull that even you – oh, it's no use. It sounds wrong. *(Urgently.)* Cyrenne, can't you realize what tonight has been like for me? I'm walking through Market Square, say, at three a.m. And suddenly there's a gigantic building slap-bang where the chip shop was – I mean, it shouldn't be there! But it is. I open the door and there's a million people I've never met. They're all smiling and they seem to want me. Lights ablaze; music blaring. And then an exciting woman *(He looks at her.)* a sweet, wonderful, exciting woman grabs my hand and hurtles me into the middle of it all. Three o'clock in the morning! And you thought there was nothing ahead but the eight o'clock buzzer. *(Sadly.)* Do you think I'm daft?

CYRENNE: Probably. *(She touches his hand.)* Are you still hungry?

PERCY: *(Rising.)* Have you found some more biscuits?

CYRENNE: *(Rising.)* I've some beans, sausage, corned beef, and more beans. Would you fancy those?

PERCY: Can a duck swim!

CYRENNE: There's still those damn dishes.

PERCY: The devil with them! You'll not see me for spray. *(He throws his raincoat on the bed and hurries into the kitchen, switching on the lights.)*

(CYRENNE follows him in and fastens the apron round him. PERCY turns on the taps and starts into the dishes with gusto.)

CYRENNE: Lot of money, fifty pounds.

PERCY: Ee, d'you have to rub it in? I'm still bleeding.

CYRENNE: A fellow could have himself a crazy holiday on fifty.

PERCY: I only spent thirty at Morecambe.

CYRENNE: Yes. Two crazy people could almost go. *(She places her fingertips to her lips and backs out of the kitchen. She sits at her dressing table, watching herself in the mirror.)* This girl in the building-that-never-was, would you take her on holiday?

PERCY: I'd need to be quick: due back at the mill on Monday.

CYRENNE: Why? Would the mill close without you?

PERCY: Ha! That'll be the day.

CYRENNE: Mmmm ...

PERCY: You may think me strange, but I enjoy washing up. I get quite a kick out of it. I like it. Most folks can't bear the sight of dirty dishes. Not me! I love it. Must be the cosiest thing in the world to have a little kitchen all your own...
(He prattles happily away.)

CURTAIN

SCENE 2

Scene – The same. Half an hour later.

There is a tray of stacked dishes on the pouffe, below the end of the bed.

When the CURTAIN rises, PERCY and CYRENNE are kneeling on the bed, facing one another, an orange balanced between their foreheads. Both are holding glasses and CYRENNE also has the whisky bottle. They are by no means drunk – not even "high"; but they are, perhaps, floating a little.

PERCY: – Idea is to travel it around our heads, turning as we go. People have rolled it miles. One who eats it, wins.

CYRENNE: To win this, you'd need a square head – and horizontal teeth.

(*The orange falls. They laugh. PERCY sits on the end of the bed.*)

PERCY: (*Pointing to the tray.*) Hey, that was the best corned-beef-bolognaise I've ever had. Didn't realize I was so peckish. Were you peckish?

CYRENNE: I was that! Liqueur, Monsewer? (*She pours whisky into his glass.*)

PERCY: Ta! I'm glad it turned out well: it's the first corned-beefbolognaise I ever cooked. (*He drinks.*) You don't do much cooking, then?

CYRENNE: Not if I see it coming. (*She raises her glass.*) Skol!

PERCY: Arrivederci!

CYRENNE: May as well finish it. (*She empties the bottle into their glasses.*) Dead men tell no tales.

PERCY: Hey up! Steady on!

CYRENNE: Now, Percival! Don't tell me you were boasting about all that liquor you drank.

PERCY: No, I had plenty – but I'm a beer-man m'self. I once drank fourteen pints at a sitting.

CYRENNE: What happened?

PERCY: I passed out. *(He grins sheepishly.)* Oh, Cyrenne, I know what I was going to ask you – oops! *(He slides from the bed to the floor.)* What college did you attend?

CYRENNE: *(Off guard.)* College?

PERCY: You said you got an M.A.

CYRENNE: Oxford.

PERCY: University, eh! Which one?

CYRENNE: One for girls, naturally.

PERCY: Magdalene?

CYRENNE: *(Sipping her whisky.)* Mm.

PERCY: Did you get an M.A. for languages?

CYRENNE: *(Shrugging.)* Various courses. I only went for fun; never did any work. Young people should have fun.

PERCY: Within reason.

CYRENNE: I did. It was all singing, dancing, and parties on the river bank. Sometimes a whole gang of us'd take out a punt and float, just float, with bottles of wine and meat pies. *(She giggles.)* David – he was an earl's son – once got the pole stuck, and we floated on leaving him like a monkey up a stick in the middle of the water.

(This is obviously something she has read in "Girls' Own", but PERCY is tremendously impressed.)

PERCY: Aye, must have been marvellous at university.

CYRENNE: He was a nice healthy boy. *(Wishfully.)* No – complications. He gave me his fraternity pin. *(She is mixing up some American college film she has seen. She balances the whisky bottle on her head.)* He had freckles and close-cropped hair, and cuddly big sweaters with stripes round the arms and "Great Britain" on the front. During semester he played trombone with a jazz group.

PERCY: What's semester?

CYRENNE: *(Vaguely.)* Oh, you know. And when I was bored we'd race down the lanes in his car, me steering and him working the pedals and playing his trombone. He wanted to marry me; but I told him he was too young. Poor David! He sulked for weeks.

(Her voice trembles slightly with emotion. She empties her whisky glass in one gulp.)

Anyway, he wasn't supposed to go with girls. It ruined his baseball or something.

PERCY: Baseball? At Oxford?

CYRENNE: *(Smoothly.)* He was American. They have baseball teams for Americans at Oxford.

PERCY: Son of an earl?

CYRENNE: That – was David. I was talking about Philip.

PERCY: Oh. I must've lost track some place. But how did you get an M.A. if you never did any work?

CYRENNE: Father bought it.

PERCY: Bought an M.A.! That doesn't seem right.

CYRENNE: You can do anything with money. Father was never short. Whenever he came to see me he always pushed a fiver in my hand. "Have fun, sweetie," he'd say.

PERCY: He sounds a very grand person. Shame he died so early: he might have – well, helped.

CYRENNE: Oh, never mind. *(She gets off the bed and rubs her back with the whisky bottle.)* Aaagh-ni-ieece!

PERCY: *(Ponderously.)* Cyrenne, do you think, perhaps, you had too much – too soon?

CYRENNE: *(Smiling.)* And you did it without a couch! *(She puts the bottle on the tray and tosses a cushion from the floor on to the chair down L.)*

PERCY: *(Rising.)* I can imagine what it's like to have been to university and all that; then strike a bit of bad luck. *(He takes out his wallet.)* So I thought – seeing your father isn't around – don't be insulted – but – *(He thrusts a five-pound note at her self-consciously.)* Have fun, sweetie! Ha ha!

CYRENNE: What's it for?

PERCY: Nothing. No strings. Go ahead!

CYRENNE: *(Taking it slowly.)* I'm afraid you've crept up behind me, Percival.

PERCY: Oh, it's for my own sake as much as anyone. Makes me feel good. First time I've ever walked beside white pillars; first time I ever felt important. *(He turns away to R, looking at his wallet.)* Not that I agree with throwing money around. Ee heck! I can't have spent all that! Phew! Must've been those clubs.

CYRENNE: That's how it goes. *(She moves across to him and gives him back the money.)*

PERCY: *(Taking it automatically.)* Thanks. *(He is about to replace it in his wallet, when he realizes.)* No! Oh, no! What's gone is gone. That's yours.

CYRENNE: OK. *(She takes it back and, crossing him, goes to hide the money in a pot on the dressing-table. She turns and tentatively offers it to him, with an instinctive jerk-back of her hand before he could even have touched it.)* There's still time.

PERCY: No, no. Just spend it wisely and – aw! Spend it how you like. S'only once in a lifetime.

CYRENNE: All gone. You've had it! There's fifty-five gone for a burton.

PERCY: I shall put it all down to experience. Shove it in the out-tray.

CYRENNE: Oh, you're not in the out-tray yet. In fact, you may yet still be *outré.* *(She hiccoughs and giggles.)* Pardon! I'm squiffy. *(She moves to him and slaps his chest.)*

(PERCY falls backwards on to the bed as he does so, his feet come up. CYRENNE catches them, and we see two large holes in his shoes.)

Doesn't mummy have your shoes mended?

PERCY: *(Rising.)* I've another pair at the digs, but brown didn't match my suit.

CYRENNE: Darling Percival, I shall dance at your wedding. From now on I'll sh-subscribe to the Scunthorpe *Bugle* or whatever's your local rag.

PERCY: Scunthorpe's not in Manchester.

CYRENNE: All right, the Manchester *Bugle*. And as soon as your wedding is announced, I'll catch the first train down – up. I'll find your church, and when they're throwing confetti, with you on the porch all flushed and tumbled, I'll shout "Oy!" *(She whistles.)* "Remember me?" *(She opens her diary and writes.)* "Percy came back!" Exclamation mark!

(PERCY takes the tray of dishes into the kitchen.)

PERCY: Bill Hedgers at the mill has a daughter sixteen and he's only thirty-six. Must be wonderful to own someone like her while you're still young: high heels, fluffy; someone you've made yourself. I envy him. Must be marvellous! Having her calling you "Dad"– asking your advice – must be marvellous! *(He picks up the pan and brush from under the sink.)*

CYRENNE: *(Writing.)* "Am going to tuck him up and take him on holiday."

(PERCY has brought the pan and brush from the kitchen. Now he sweeps crumbs off the carpet.)

PERCY: I often imagine myself with a daughter, but never a wife. S'funny! I see myself as a widower; my wife has died young. I never bother how; she's just dead. This is on me long walks round town. I see myself with this baby: bathing it, and feeding it, and tickling it, and changing its nappies – I've never told anyone else this. Next she's off to school. I've got on by this time. I'm successful, important, grey round the temples – and I collect her in the car. One of those whoppers, you know, all wheels and straps round the bonnet. *(He takes the pan and brush back into the kitchen.)* Then she comes home with her first boyfriend – and I start worrying! I have to shake my head and think of something else.

CYRENNE: Have you a dog at home, or a cat?

PERCY: No, why?

CYRENNE: It's something to love. *(She writes.)* "Good old Ginger!!" Double exclamation mark. *(She snaps the diary shut.)*

PERCY: What're you writing in there?

CYRENNE: The opening chapter of Percy, my latest book.

PERCY: I think you're marvellous. Phew! Poems and painting...!

(CYRENNE picks up his jacket and helps him into it.)

What about the washing up?

CYRENNE: It's Sunday. 'Gainst the law to wash up on a Sunday. I heard of one man who did it and some of his dirty-minded friends never spoke to him again. *(She leads him L.)*

PERCY: Where're we going?

CYRENNE: You must learn to ignore the tea-leaves till you need the pot again. *(She pushes him into the chair L.)* You may've died by the next meal and you'd've wasted minutes of life round the dustbin.

(Kneeling R of him, she pulls off one of his shoes.)

PERCY: What're you doing?

(CYRENNE takes off his other one, then rises and shows him the holes. She drops the shoes into his lap.)

CYRENNE: Once more around the block, dear friend, and you'd've been down to stocking feet. Now for slippers! I should have some.

(CYRENNE exits down L.)

PERCY: Where've you gone?

CYRENNE: *(Off.)* Rummaging for slippers.

PERCY: *(Suspiciously.)* Men's slippers?

CYRENNE: *(Off.)* What else?

PERCY: *(Darkly.)* Whose are they?

(CYRENNE enters down L with a newspaper, a pair of scissors, and two paper bags.)

CYRENNE: Mr Green the Fruiterer's. *(She puts a bag on each of PERCY's feet and stands back to survey the result.)* Mm. Very sexy! *(She takes a cushion from the chair behind him, places it on the floor R of his chair and sits. During the ensuing dialogue she cuts the paper and fits it into his shoes. Casually.)* Been on holiday this year?

PERCY: Yes. I went to Morecambe. Went with Ginger and his wife'n kids. They have friends over there, you know. But I stayed in digs.

CYRENNE: Otherwise all right?

PERCY: Yes, I had a marvellous time. Saw all the shows; did a bit of swimming; and I went horse-riding one day; first time I've done it. And there's some beautiful walks round there. One day I went...

CYRENNE: By yourself?

PERCY: Pardon?

CYRENNE: By yourself?

PERCY: No, I went with people from the digs. There were a lot of married couples there. They took a fancy to me. I was always making them laugh. No, it was marvellous! I think I'll go somewhere else next year, though.

CYRENNE: Good.

PERCY: What about you? Did you – I mean, do you ... *(He stops.)*

CYRENNE: Yes, we're allowed holidays.

PERCY: *(Sorry.)* Oh heck.

CYRENNE: 'S all right! Have you any more weeks coming?

PERCY: No, I've had my whack. Hey! Fancy you sitting there doing that.

CYRENNE: Just fancy!

PERCY: Being domesticated. You!

CYRENNE: God help us, here we go again! Will you please stop treating me like some sort of freak.

PERCY: *(Piqued.)* Well, I'm sorry; but it's not one-sided you know! If you stopped treating me like a yokel with straw hair and a patch on me arse...! I shouldn't have said that. I'm sorry.

CYRENNE: Damn it, love, that's what I mean! If you feel like saying "arse", say it! We've all got one.

PERCY: *(Pompously.)* The fact remains I do not consider it necessary for a gentleman to be uncouth in the presence of a lady.

(CYRENNE laughs helplessly, but PERCY remains on his dignity.)

If I accidentally make a blunt remark with a lady present, I apologize; I'll say no more.

CYRENNE: Next Sunday the Epistle of St Percy!

(There is a silence, broken only by the snip-snip of CYRENNE's scissors. PERCY, face set dogmatically, thinks over the past few sentences. Five seconds later a tiny smile twitches his lips. He kills it and has a quick look at CYRENNE. He thinks for another five seconds and the smile returns; he frowns hard in an effort to remain serious. This becomes impossible. He chokes back a chuckle; then another; and another. CYRENNE looks up, and he loses the battle.)

PERCY: *(Between chuckles.)* You aren't half rude! "We've all got one!" *(He roars with laughter.)*

CYRENNE: *(Calmly.)* Oh, I slay 'em.

PERCY: *(Wiping his eyes.)* Oh dear, oh dear, oh dear! *(He blows his nose.)* I've had some real good fun tonight. I have!

CYRENNE: There you are, Killer! *(She gives him his shoes.)*

PERCY: Ta. Thanks very much. *(He puts on his shoes.)*

(CYRENNE rises and crosses to R to put the scissors on the dressing-table, and the paper in the waste-paper basket.)

CYRENNE: You know, love, you remind me of a paper bag.

PERCY: S'funny thing to say.

CYRENNE: But you do. You remind me of a carrier bag; one of those old-fashioned ones with thick string-and-wood handles. Winthram's Drapery Store: brown and solid, until one day it carries a liberty bodice, and it crackles and giggles. Would you like to come on holiday.

PERCY: Oh, aye! When do we go? Today?

CYRENNE: Yes, or tomorrow. *(She returns to sit on the cushion R of him.)*

(PERCY laughs.)

Would you?

PERCY: With you?

CYRENNE: Mm.

PERCY: Nothing I'd like better.

CYRENNE: Will you come then?

PERCY: Seriously?

CYRENNE: Very seriously.

PERCY: I couldn't.

CYRENNE: The mill won't close without you.

PERCY: No, but ...

CYRENNE: Afraid?

PERCY: Me? Why should I be?

CYRENNE: Because of what mummy would say; and the boss; and the lady next door.

PERCY: Did you mean for us – to go together, sort of – together?

CYRENNE: You'd be my Sunday boy, Percy. You'd have everything I've saved from the rest of the world. Just a week; no strings on my side. Then I'd wave you off at the coach station, and we'd both have something – well, something nice for...

PERCY: For when the eight o'clock buzzer goes!

CYRENNE: Will you come?

PERCY: What about money? I'm not rich.

CYRENNE: Ginger's paying.

PERCY: Eh? Oh, yes! *(He savours the idea.)* Oogh, what I wouldn't give! See that plum in Ginger's mouth: it'd shrivel to a currant! *(He rises and moves C, shaking his head.)* It's a cheeky idea. It is truly; but I couldn't possibly. I mean, it's winter. I've had my two weeks this year.

CYRENNE: *(Rising.)* They weren't exactly a success though, were they? *(She moves to replace the cushion on the chair.)*

PERCY: Who said so?

CYRENNE: You did, between the lines.

(PERCY begins to bluster, then gives in and nods.)

PERCY: I must be pretty obvious. It wasn't too good. Never is. I don't enjoy Christmas much, either.

CYRENNE: *(Moving to stand by him.)* Well?

PERCY: I'm trembling inside. 'Fact is, I don't have much confidence in myself, d'you follow? I've left it a bit late. I'm not thirtyfive. I'm – I'm forty-two. Another six months I'll be forty-three. I don't think I could come up to your expectations. I know I can't. I'm not going on holiday to be ridiculed the first time we – if you'll excuse me – go into the bedroom. I'm being blunt, but there it is.

(He crosses her to up L.) You've arrived too late. You know how youngsters when they're growing up have pimples? Well, I had pimples – my face was covered in them. They lasted until I was twenty-six, and unfortunately I didn't have the right personality to rise above them. Then they suddenly cleared away – almost overnight. An Army doctor gave me a course of dieting. Very good man. So! I thought I'd be OK with girls at last. *(He shakes his head.)*

Believe me, I might just as well've kept the pimples. At least I'd've had an excuse.

CYRENNE: Supposing I told you – some of the things I say... *(She bites her lip and stops.)* Oh, take a chance, Percy! Why not? Percy?

(PERCY swings to face her and the words tumble out.)

PERCY: Because I'm afraid I'm not a man; I'm afraid I'm effeminate or something. Everyone I know's been married, and had children, and – I'm scared of finding there's something different about me. Oh, I know I should grab a chance to prove myself but – I'm afraid to. I'm afraid.

CYRENNE: There's nothing different about you, love. I'm the expert.

PERCY: Oh, well, there's still the mill on Monday.

(CYRENNE sits on the end oj the bed, speaking more to herself than to him.)

CYRENNE: I wanted to go on holiday. I'd have liked to go to
   Switzerland; but anywhere would've done: Morcambe,
   BIackpool, Potter's Bar.

   (There is a pause. PERCY moves to her.)

PERCY: Have you a railway guide?

CYRENNE: Yes. Somewhere.

PERCY: Go and fetch it. We'll try Blackpool. *(He sits L of her
   on the bed.)* I'll spend tonight at the hotel and bring my
   bag round first thing tomorrow. I've enough clothes for
   a week, if you don't mind rubbing through a couple of
   shirts for me.

   (CYRENNE nods.)

   And would you not starch the collars, please? It cuts my
   neck.

CYRENNE: No starch.

PERCY: Oh, and a pair of socks, if you'd kindly rub through
   those, an' all.

CYRENNE: No starch!

   *(PERCY laughs. Then summoning all his courage, he leans forward
   and pecks her cheek. CYRENNE responds by drawing his face close
   to hers; she kisses him purposefully and very professionally.)*

   (Rising and crossing down L.) We'll buy some shirts. I
   need one or two things in any case. Now! Where is that
   timetable?

   *(CYRENNE exits down L. PERCY sits for a long time thinking,
   and relishing her kiss. Slowly he relaxes. His optimism grows, then
   blooms into exuberance. He jumps up, slaps his fists, rubs his hands,
   laughs, cries, and at one point does a happy little shuffling dance,
   ending by swinging round in a circle. This movement brings him
   face to face with the bed. His confidence evaporates and he turns
   slowly away, frowning and biting the edge of his thumb. He walks
   to the dressing-table mirror and gazes at himself.)*

PERCY: Oh, it'll be all right, lad. Don't worry. Just take it easy! I'll do it. I must. I will.

(The telephone rings. PERCY answers it.)

Hello? *(He consults the number on the dial.)* Yes? ... Um, I beg pardon, sir? ... Father? ... Whose father? ... Yes, righto. *(He hangs up and slumps on to the bed. He seems lost – dumbfounded.)*

(CYRENNE enters down L, an open railway guide in her hands. She crosses to RC.)

CYRENNE: This is printed in Latin, it's so old. Who was it?

(PERCY does not reply.)

Darling, the phone! Who was it?

PERCY: It was your father, back from the dead.

(CYRENNE stops in her tracks.)

CYRENNE: You mean my stepfather.

(PERCY remains on the bed, his back to her.)

PERCY: When did your real father die?

CYRENNE: Long time ago ...

PERCY: And your mother married again!

CYRENNE: Yes.

(PERCY rises and swings to face her. He is puzzled and angry because of it.)

PERCY: You said your mother died when you were twelve. *(He strides into the kitchen, switches on the light, finds her rent book over the cooker, and reads out the name from the cover.)* "Miss C. Duponitrades."

(CYRENNE moves L.)

Now it's making sense. *(He throws the book down, turns out the light, and returns to the bedroom.)* Since when has there been a Greek brigadier in the British Army?

CYRENNE: *(Sitting down L.)* Who said he was in the British Army?

PERCY: That man said he was your father – he talked with a foreign accent – said he was ringing from the cafe. Yes! Your father runs a cafe with your brother. Right!

CYRENNE: *(Defiantly.)* Well done! Full marks.

PERCY: *(Pacing to R and C; angrily.)* A rent book for a house you own; nannies and French marchionesses; an M.A. your father bought! Did you ever go to Oxford? Come on, the truth! Did you?

CYRENNE: I slopped in a dismal little kitchen from leaving school till I was twenty.

PERCY: And I swallowed it wholesale! Phew! Intricate details of parties on the river, and – and a brother-in-law who's a surgeon! And what about your mother? Is she alive, too?

CYRENNE: Yes, yes, yes, she's alive! Satisfied?

PERCY: That's something I'll never forgive. Your own flesh and blood – to say they were *dead*! That's awful. Aren't they good enough? Is that it? Just a little Italian couple, or Greek or whatever it is?

CYRENNE: I tried to explain once. Oh, it doesn't matter.

PERCY: Oh, no, it doesn't matter! It proves what a yob I am. Real gormless, that's me! You poked fun at everything I did. I couldn't even visit the bathroom without getting a belly laugh! But you were so clever, that's what gets me. I shed tears over you and your poor old brigadier – gave you five pounds to laugh at me!

CYRENNE: It was your own idea.

PERCY: I know; and I'll tell you another. You'll curl up at this. If the holiday had gone well I was thinking of marriage. You and me! Isn't that funny! *(He moves up R.)*

CYRENNE: Oh, do me a favour, love! I know better; the first morning you'd have crawled off with your tail between your legs.

PERCY: Would I really?

CYRENNE: Yes, Percy.

PERCY: Would I! Would I! We'll see! *(He flings the cover off the bed.)* I'm as good as you any time. I'm better!

(CYRENNE makes no reply.)

What're you waiting for? More money? Get undressed!

(CYRENNE turns to look at him, then slowly rises and crosses to the dressing-table.)

CYRENNE: *(Quietly.)* All right. *(Deliberately she takes off her necklace and then her earrings.)*

(PERCY lowers his eyes and swings away, there are tears in his voice:)

PERCY: Oh, shut up and leave me alone!

(CYRENNE moves up and leans on the tallboy up R. PERCY sits again, hunched on the L side of the bed.)

CYRENNE: You can't shame me – unfortunately.

PERCY: Everything's crumpled – just gone and crumpled. I had this feeling – wonderful – I thought you were so exciting – because I'm lonely. So damned lonely! Oh, what's the use! *(Rising, he takes his coat and scarf from the hooks and walks to the door up L.)* I'd best be going. But I can't tell you how I wish I'd never answered that telephone.

CYRENNE: Would you like a heavenly chorus?

PERCY: Pardon?

CYRENNE: You could do a Charlie Chaplin down the middle of Euston Road: shuffling over the brow, the traffic lights blinking mistily. What a bloody fuss! *(Moving RC, she kicks off her shoes and shuffles into her slippers.)*

PERCY: There's no call for swearing. It's not clever.

(But the fish wife comes out in CYRENNE.)

CYRENNE: You come here in a stupor, find you've no guts, and you're ashamed – until I mention an M.A., a butler, and the fact I was sired by a brigadier.

PERCY: Yes, all lies.

CYRENNE: Listen, love, if I've told you the moon's green or God's a woman, I'm still the same person you appreciated ten minutes ago. So stuff that up your mill chimney! *(She takes off her stockings, resting each foot in turn on the dressing-table stool.)*

PERCY: Oh, no! I'll not have that! You're not the same to me.

CYRENNE: Because you're a snob, a one hundred per cent, cast iron, elastic-belted snob!

PERCY: *(Moving down L.)* Not at all!

CYRENNE: Yes, you are, with your "Ee by gums" and your "Up for the Cups!"

PERCY: Oh, sticks and stones!

CYRENNE: Your little British belly pumped with excitement at the thought of mixing with gentility, even to the extent of a gentle whore like me. *(She crosses L trying to unzip her dress.)*

PERCY: Just – just watch your language!

CYRENNE: As soon as I establish a true-blue background you're thrilled and oh-so-terribly impressed.

(CYRENNE exits down L, but returns immediately, moving up to him.)

You kiss my feet, cook my supper, and set up some kind of mission tent in my parlour. Unzip the back!

PERCY: What're you doing?

CYRENNE: Going to bed. What else? You use my flat and my time to bolster what's left of a tatty weekend; even go off and come back for more! *(She moves to the door down L.)* Seven times round the block planning my redemption! But not once asking yourself if I care a pig's bottom what you plan.

(CYRENNE exits down L, taking off her frock.)

PERCY: Oh, lovely! Lovely! Lovely words for a young lady! *(He moves up R and yells back across the bed.)* Any planning that was done, you did! You planned me out of five quid and a holiday – at the end of which, no doubt, you'd have planned me out of everything else – premium bonds, the lot! *(He moves to the doorway down L.)* I count myself very lucky – very lucky indeed! Are you listening?

(CYRENNE enters down L, buttoning her pyjamas jacket. They are men's pyjamas of bright orange. She crosses to the dressing-table.)

CYRENNE: – I don't give a galloping damn if you disappear in circles or hang yourself in your Lancashire cotton drawers. My life is my own! *(Deliberately she pulls off her right eyelashes.)* And I live as I please. *(She removes her left eyelashes.)* Every two-bit hero thinks he has a right to reorganize me. Bloody marvellous! *(She thickly covers her face in cleansing cream, then removes her make-up with tissues.)*

PERCY: I've asked you to watch your lang –

CYRENNE: There's the door! Nobody's keeping you. Go on! Slam it and shout, "Bum" through the keyhole!

PERCY: By heck! *(He leans against the door up L.)*

CYRENNE: There's one comes round here. I'll tell you! Once a week I hear him creeping down the steps; I hear him breathing while he's prising up the letter-box flap – to shout through it – to scream and slobber filthy words at me.

PERCY: Well, he's to be pitied.

(The slanging match is over. They are both calm now.)

CYRENNE: The lies I tell are useful to me. They're old friends, the people I invent. I laugh with them and cry with them. You think you are lonely? You've a mummy back home waiting to pack your rattle and fold your scarf all ready for next year. I bet she's baking a cake this very minute. And what about your father?

PERCY: He works at the mill.

CYRENNE: Old pals together! On one of my birthdays I was admiring myself in the mirror; wasn't wearing much. My stepfather came in without knocking. After an unpatriotic incident I won't bother to shock you with, I left home. *(She rises.)* Are you with me so far, Padre?

PERCY: Yes.

(CYRENNE sits on the R side of the bed and kicks off her slippers.)

CYRENNE: You see, my stepfather, well, he wasn't a good stepdaddy – *(She clambers into bed.)* so, I started pretending I was someone else's daughter – usually a character in the book I was reading. I was always reading. I read *What Katy Did* and what she did next. Oh, I swallowed the lot, from Dickens to *Lady Chatterley* – at which point, Padre, I gave up reading. I examined my assets from the front, back, to the side, and I said, "Cyrenne! You've struck oil!" *(She plumps her pillow.)* Next comes a dismal romance lasting one year and two days, and ending with my fiance in jail for slashing his wife – the wife he hadn't mentioned. He still writes to me, complaining about the food. Then I was a nurse, then a typist, shop assistant, hostess, and finally – well, as for the rest of my saga – I deserve a bloody M.A.! *(She hurls a spare pillow at him.)* So! – now and then I lunch with Lady This or That, spend twenty pounds an ounce on Woolworth's fragrant scent, or race down Oxford lanes with my dashing virgin boy. And when the going's rough, the brigadier is there with lovely tales of Samarkand or Rumblejumblepore. No, I don't give a toot what anyone thinks. I have a goddam wonderful life. So Good night, Children, Everywhere! *(She flops back and draws the sheets over her head.)*

PERCY: Phew! You don't half cuss! Bet you could beat Ginger if you really tried.

(CYRENNE rises and, without looking at him, goes into the kitchen. PERCY follows to RC. CYRENNE gets a glass of water and returns. She passes Percy with a sniff, demurely holding the collar of her pyjama jacket, and makes a wide circle around him, getting into bed at the L side.)

CYRENNE: I thought you'd gone back to Scunthorpe.

PERCY: It's Manchester; you know perfectly well.

CYRENNE: Oh. *(Placing the glass on the bedside table, she snuggles under the sheets.)*

PERCY: They suit you, those pyjamas. You look quite nice. *(He clears his throat.)* As I said before ...

CYRENNE: *(Muffled.)* And you'll say again!

PERCY: I beg your pardon?

(CYRENNE sits bolt upright and looks at him with a heavy sigh.)

CYRENNE: Are you coming to bed or aren't you?

PERCY: Eh?

CYRENNE: You heard.

She smiles, a perkily quizzical smile. PERCY opens and shuts his mouth in pompous changes of mind before capitulating into a huge, hopeful smirk. He takes the brave plunge – chin clamped!

Setting aside his rattle, PERCY whips off his raincoat and lays it carefully upon a chair. Tidily he adds his jacket, his scarf, then positions his shoes precisely on the floor. After removing his unbuttoned trousers in a hopping circle, he places them fussily upon his other clothing. He un-winds his necktie –

– and begins to roll it neatly – (the heck with it!). He hurls the necktie high over his shoulder, and approaches CYRENNE in shirt, socks and underpants.

CYRENNE holds out her arms. All is so promising – until PERCY loses confidence and slumps hopelessly on the bed's edge.

PERCY: Oh I don't know. I'll have to think about it.

CURTAIN

ACT I

CYRENNE (PAGE 37)

CYRENNE: Yes?

BILL: Hello, Cyrenne – sweetheart!

CYRENNE: Hello, Willie –darling!

BILL: Darling yourself. How's tricks?

CYRENNE: All right; and you?

BILL: Got a cold.

CYRENNE: *(Laughing intimately.)* Well, you shouldn't run about with nothing on.

BILL: You suggested it.

CYRENNE: I did no such thing.

BILL: Strip poker was your idea.

CYRENNE: Oh, no! It was your idea. *(To PERCY.)* Don't break anything, will you, love.

BILL: Say that again?

CYRENNE: I wasn't talking to you, Willie.

BILL: Is someone there?

CYRENNE: Yes. Jealous?

BILL: Madly. Who is it?

CYRENNE: Mind your own business!

BILL: Feel like a party tonight?

CYRENNE: Go to a party tonight?

BILL: Yes. Now. Pronto!

CYRENNE: What sort of party?

BILL: You'd turn up a trip on a yacht?

CYRENNE: Yacht? What kind of yacht?

BILL: A real yacht. Lap lap.

CYRENNE: I've never been to a party on a yacht.

BILL: Weakening, Sweetie?

CYRENNE: Hang on! *(To PERCY.)* Do you really want to stay?

PERCY: I don't want to stop you having ...

CYRENNE: I asked you if you wanted to stay.

PERCY: Yes. But I mean ...

CYRENNE: Whatever happens?

PERCY: How d'you mean?

CYRENNE: *(Smiling, then speaks into receiver.)* No go, Willie! My boyfriend won't let me.

BILL: Which boyfriend?

PERCY: No, wait a minute!

CYRENNE: Ssssh! *(Into phone.)* What did you say?

BILL: Which boyfriend?

CYRENNE: Oh, he's just a fellow who does the washing-up. G'bye.

(She replaces the receiver.)

ACT II

PERCY (PAGE 52)

PERCY: Hello? Is that the Pablo Private Hotel, please?

VOICE: It's the Pablo. Yes, that's right.

PERCY: Oh. This is Mr Winthram. Has Mr Grappley returned yet, please?

VOICE: Grappley? Dunno. I'll find out.

PERCY: Thank you. *(To himself.)* Fighting time now; and I'm too damn scared to wind the clock ... Oh, what if he's not back? What if he's plastered down some alley?

GINGER: Hello?

PERCY: Hello, Ginge! It's Perce.

GINGER: Speak up!

PERCY: Perce.

GINGER: Hello, love! How'd you make out?

PERCY: Fine. I got on fine.

GINGER: Did you do it?

PERCY: I er, came home with her, yes.

GINGER: I know; but you're not still there?

PERCY: Yes.

GINGER: Bluddy-'ell! What've you been doing?

PERCY: Talking.

GINGER: Talking! Is that all?

PERCY: It's all so far, yes.

GINGER: Ha ha! Get your wallet!

PERCY: Ginge, listen! Don't you think it's a bit stupid, all this?

GINGER: Ha, I've won! No backing out!

92

PERCY: I'm not backing out at all. Frankly I'm giving you a chance. I mean, I'm here. I'm here, Ginge! Just a matter of time, that's all ... Hello?

GINGER: I'm here.

PERCY: D'you still want to go through with it, then?

GINGER: You've lost! You're done! You're dead scared! *(He hangs up.)*

PERCY: Who's dead scared. Ha! ... Hello? ... Hello? ... Ginger? ... *(He hangs up.)*

CYRENNE (PAGE 65)

CYRENNE: Yes?

BILL: Cyrenna-mia?

CYRENNE: Yes.

BILL: It's Romeo, sweetheart!

CYRENNE: Willie-darling, hello!

BILL: We're just starting out.

CYRENNE: Starting out for where?

BILL: For the yacht, sugar. Change your mind and come.

CYRENNE: No thanks, love. I've been on the Queen Mary. *(Urgently.)*

Come round here instead.

BILL: And miss free champagne?

CYRENNE: *Please*, Willie. *Please.* Come and see me, Willie. Please come over.

BILL: Sorry. It's me for the Skylark.

CYRENNE: You'll be seasick.

BILL: Come with me, and we'll bring up the past together.

CYRENNE: Yes. *(Dully.)* Some other time. *(She hangs up.)*

PERCY: Hello?

PAPA: Bays-a-water seven-seven-nothings-seven?

PERCY: *(Checking number.)* Yes?

PAPA: I am wishing-a speak-a to Ricky. Yes? No, no? Tell-a Ricky, pliss. Papa is-a waiting.

PERCY: Um ... I beg pardon, sir?

PAPA: Ah! Is-a not Ricky. Ohkay! Pliss to ring later. Yes? Am-a the old father. Papa Duponitrades.

PERCY: Father?

PAPA: Si-si.

PERCY: Whose father?

PAPA: Cyrenna is-a my daughter. She's the good girl. Am speak from the cafe. Yes? Ohkay? Will ringa later. Bye-bye. Ohkay? *(He rings off.)*

PERCY: Yes, righto. *(He hangs up.)*

MOTHER ADAM

UNLIKELY MOTHER AND ONLY SON

Miss Bushnell was crocheted in cardigan-heaven with bright button eyes, grey-bun hair and discreet legs in flat shoes. She ran theatrical digs at 11 Paradise Square in the City of Spires. When first I played Oxford, Miss Bushnell offered feather beds, hearty breakfasts, tasty lunches, crumpet teas, and after-show bubble-and-squeak. All for £2 weekly!

'Bushy' was motherly and tiny. Her gas-lit terrace house was teeny, too, with scant space for mice, yet somehow she accommodated two or three actors. No bathroom comes to mind: just boiled water in ewers, and an alfresco privy in whitewash at yard's end. Finest digs ever! *All found for two pound.* Bushy's heart was legendary, her cooking superb, and her Guests a parade of stars-gone-by or those-to-be. A forgotten Owen Nares lodged there. Charles Laughton. Noel Coward. Laurence Olivier. Ralph Richardson 1922. Elsa Lanchester 1928. And humble me in '48. Bushy's Visitors Book was traditionally flowery:

> 'Our hearts are yours, oh Empress Lady of Lands.'
> 'Adieu, Adieu, esteemed Bubble-and-Squeak.'

Once, Miss Bushnell wondered if she might presume upon my goodness for an errand of mercy; would I deliver a cloth-shrouded-bowl of custard to a bed-ridden lady? Miss Bushnell made dense custard, usefully, and I wobbled it a mile via St. Giles to a dilapidated mansion where bell-pushes mushroomed beside the curling, rusted-pinned cards of forsaken professors and other such leathery souls.

A resplendent Admiral answered the bed-ridden lady's bell. Plumed hat. Epaulettes. White gloves. Drawn sword! Adam was his name, and my custard was 'manna indeed' –

' – Do present it thyself, Sire. Visitors are rare. Mammles will adore your company.'

Sire? ... Thyself? ... Mammles?

Adam saluted, vertical steel at forehead, then sheathed his blade. He beckoned and I followed him up deteriorating stairs, up, out of worn mahogany past frayed-carpet's end, up into peeling pine where pipes gurgled and pigeons cooed. Admiral Adam cooed, too, outside an attic door:

'Viszy-wizzy-tors, Mammles.' *(Confidential whisper.)* 'Mother may be on the potty.'

'Ah.'

We waited. My custard waxed heavy. Adam raised clenched knuckles to his lips and squinted at me with strangely anxious, almost frightened eyes. I sensed a tiddly shiver of my own at Mammles' signal: three knocks of her Black Rod on the Devil's Floor.

'Here we come a-diddle, Mammles. Custy-wustard.'

Arthritic Mammles was propped in a bamboo bed, stage-centre of a bamboo room, an over-rouged prima donna in flannelette nightie. She wore a sequined toque skewered into rat-tails of milky-grey hair. *Grotesque.* Down-casting my glance from her crippled hands, I bowed butler-wise then set her custard on a bamboo table. Mammles smiled sorely through a grimace:

'Kindly convey my gratitude to your Bushy-Woman. She is rare in an evil world. I sacrificed my Body to the Ungodly. *(Shrieking.)* Forty Years for Jesus among heathens.'

Adam screeched back at her, 'Oh God Almighty!' Wild-eyed, he tore open his collar then slumped on a bamboo stool, admiral's hat askew, sword a-clatter. An unveiled costumiers' label dangled at his neck: 'SWORD NOT INCLUDED.' Mammles snorted:

'That is my son. Born for everlasting contempt. *(To me.)* Very well. You may leave!'

I did so on a stammered *'b-bye-bye'* with a fatuous wave. From outside on the landing I thought I heard Adam weeping 'oh-God-oh-God-oh-God', a lonely sobbing, sad to hear.

* * *

My darling wife Fiona and I have been married fifty years. We love the City of Spires. We met as youngsters during a Season at the Oxford Playhouse. There, I directed one of my early potboilers *Poison In Jest.* July 1957. Fiona was my leading lady, and Harold Pinter acted the sinister Chauffeur. ('Didn't know *he* fancied writing plays.') Fiona and I began walking-out from the Playhouse; wandering in summer meadows, 'lemonades' at the Trout; boating on the Isis. For old times sake, I took Fiona to meet Miss Bushnell. 'Couldn't find her! Gone!

No trace! No Miss Bushnell nor even hint of a Paradise Square.

I swear Miss Bushnell was real. I swear. Yet, perchance, only a smidgin of Mammles was truly bamboo and the rest a bamboozle of memories decked in mischief, heady prisms twisting bitter lemon into hot orange and fetching golden moments out of the blue. Was there ever a boarding house Admiral with a sword? Truly? – or is Adam a dramatic fib revamped into the second duologue for my Lonely Trilogy?

Beginners please!

* * *

MOTHER ADAM

The Unlikely Mother's name is MAMMLES
ADAM is the name of her Only Son

Mother Adam was produced on Tour
by Flint-Shipman & Torwood Productions in 1971.

Subsequently presented by Kamiro Productions & Stage Seventy
Limited at the Arts Theatre, London, in December 1971 with Roy
Dotrice and Beatrix Lehman, directed by Charles Dyer.

* * *

Paul Elliott and Duncan C. Weldon presented Hermione Baddeley
in a new Tour which opened in January 1973 at the Shakespeare
Memorial Theatre, Stratford-Upon-Avon. Peter Wyngarde played
Adam. Directed by Charles Dyer.

* * *

The Play is in Two Acts during a Sunday evening of 1950s
England.

We are in the gone-to-seed attic of a Victorian mansion.

The action is more or less continuous.

ACT ONE

Arthritic MAMMLES sits humped in bed, her arms folded over twisted fingers. Behind her is an attic window through which we see clouds, roofs and chimneys. MAMMLES' eyes are swivelled towards a mirror high on a bamboo hatstand. She watches reflections of the street below – her only contact with Outside, unless an act of God rips away her ceiling.

Littering the attic are grotesque souvenirs from farthest hither and thither; but even stranger are the polka dots, stripes and shades with which ADAM has decorated his mother's little world.

Church bells are ringing and children's voices singing: "Yes Jesus Loves Me." These sounds fade away ...

MAMMLES: Adam. Adam! There is a smudge on St Peter's. A smudge. And I am missing the graveyard. Vibration. My mirror, Adam!

> *ADAM rises from behind the bed head – with a pot of enamel and a brush. He wears his Russian pyjama top over trousers, and looks like a parson – which he is not. He adjusts MAMMLES' mirror.*

Those wagons in the night, Adam. Oh monsters, rumbling monsters. Three of them, and lights. Twisting blue lights. I like vibration. A kind of pain. But it lives, Adam... No! On the lateral, Adam. Nudge it! No! The graveyard is smudged. That weeping angel is blurred.

> *ADAM rubs the mirror with a tugged pyjama sleeve.*

Ah, that sidesman has arrived. He is primping over your ear. Homosexual, that sidesman is. Homosexual.

> *(ADAM stoops to focus the Sidesman. He turns to MAMMLES puzzled; then peeps comically through the back window, gazing downwards...)*

Too proud for godliness, that Sidesman. See his neck and shoulders. Hate that Sidesman's neck.

(ADAM moves R. for his paint and brush. He continues round, below the bed to D. L.

En route he pauses and peers at the Audience Wall – as though into a mirror. He examines his back view; then scrapes at a front tooth with his finger nail ... sucks ... leans closer to the 'mirror', and scrapes again.)

– Here come the harlots! Reeking of parfum d'amour and talcum. Camouflaging their lust at matins. See!

(MAMMLES eases her neck upwards, straining to see further in the mirror.)

– Twittering at that homosexual Sidesman now! *(She shouts.)* Wasting your time, Jezebels.

(MAMMLES catches sight of ADAM who is surveying the room for fresh subjects. ADAM's eye falls upon a shrouded Box below MAMMLES' bed.)

(Warningly.) Adam!

(But ADAM is deep in his creative urge; un-hearing. He places his paint and brush on the floor, and whips away the dark cover ...

... to reveal MAMMLES' Box. An impressive Edwardian travelling trunk. Blue–black hide; brass-bound; gleamling as a guardsman's saddlery; seeming sacred in its 'un-paintedness'!

Just as ADAM is about to stoop for his paint and brush...)

MAMMLES: Adam! Not My Box. *You will not decorate My Box!*

(ADAM nods gloomily; adopts a humorous sulky expression. He stands hugging the Box cover, gazing indecisively about the room.

MAMMLES returns to her commentary.)

– Clutching, giggling; plucking his sleeve! Maggots suckling a cankered limb. I remember a Dutch trader. New Guinea. Three days injured in a swamp; his foot waxing putrid. My brother Caleb and me heated a knife – lanced his flesh; and Maggots oozed. *(With relish.)* *Maggots*! – oozing like those shameless women crowding that Sidesman.

(ADAM nods unmoved. He swings the Box cover over his shoulders, college gown-style. And he moves down to admire his effect in the audience mirror.)

– Now here's a perpetual one in satin! I despise her limp wrist and tight shining buttocks.

(Down Left, the Water Tank area is piled with books, newspapers, and great family Bible; and a portable gramophone, records, etc. ADAM takes a record-sleeve and places it upon his head – it has the atmosphere of a mortar board.)

ADAM: You Children! – rampant in your pot and puberty, gamboling in stereophonic bliss, bare-chested, bare groined. And me! – who sniffed and shuffled in red-flannel gloom. You Children! – all-knowing, brassy-eyed, where once I blushed and faltered –

MAMMLES: – I will take my breakfast now, Adam.

ADAM: And these leather grannies! –

(ADAM indicates his Mother...)

– who chatter imperturbably of loins, brothels, buttocks, and homosexuality. *Homosexuality*! – unknown in the Forties, Children. Postponed for the War, you know. Nationally, the Germans were stuck with it; the French ignored it; Americans refused to believe it – ; and we English reserved it strictly for upper classes.

(ADAM strikes a fresh pose.)

Undergraduates tinkered, and dryly debated it during those symposiums; high school girls puzzled over rumours; but suburban daughters – Sir – never!

(ADAM raises an eyebrow at his reflection.)

Indeed, whereas Plato may have been straddled and Tibetans riddled, Nineteen-Thirties Anglo-Saxons lived and died having contentedly floated past it. Yet you Children! – *and my Mother*, who emerged from the womb through an iron mangle on to oilcloth; she, who spread

God's word to heathens, who walked as a nun among lepers, who strode Bible-aloft through the down-trodden of Hackney – she nonchalantly dismisses a satin lady for obscenity, and accuses the Sidesman of buggery. Class dismissed!

(ADAM removes his 'gown'. He goes to MAMMLES' Box...)

Is my father folded in here, Mammles? Not withering pigskin, I mean; but whispering in a forgotten letter? Or pipe-smoking on a yellowed snapshot?

(ADAM knocks on the Box lid.)

Are you in there, Dad?

MAMMLES: Cover the Box, Adam. Cover it!

ADAM: I was only wondering.

MAMMLES: Or *wandering*, Adam!

ADAM: Yes yes. Wandering. Very droddle, Mammles-love. Very droddle.

MAMMLES: That stethoscope, Adam, – take it back to your Museum, did you? Or are we still playing doctors?

ADAM: *(Returning to the bed-head.)* I do not *play* during my ah-mental vacations. *I am.* Just then I was addressing a Senate of young ladies. I was particularly brilliant, handsome, intellectual, and sexually desirable. Every sighing maiden tingled to share my bed...

(ADAM addresses the audience mirror.)

– and I thank you, sweet ladies. You have excited my Sunday. Let us now do likewise for my mother's!

(He consults a list pinned to the back wall.)

Um – calisthenics, and then breakfast: Yes, Mammles?

MAMMLES: No.

ADAM: *Yes!* Mustn't miss our 'Up across then laterals'. Um – performed our other little chores, have we?

MAMMLES: Yes.

ADAM: Aha. Take your word for it. Newspapers; milk. Yes.
Um – good! Oh – did I kiss you this muddle? No!
Strange. There is a kind of different Sundayishness.

(He kisses MAMMLES' forehead; then returns to the list.)

Good muddle, Mammles. How are you this muddle?

MAMMLES: I will not be patronised, Adam.

ADAM: Oh heddle forbiddle.

MAMMLES: I wish to see your face, Adam! Your face!

*(MAMMLES is unable to twist her neck far; she may swivel her eyes
only. ADAM side-steps downstage into her line of vision.)*

You are simple, Adam. Never grew up.

ADAM: Yes, Mammles. I am an imbecile. What am I? – An
imbecile.

MAMMLES: I *will* have respect. My brain is young; and my
– and my –

ADAMS: – Wisdom, intellect, maturity, integrity; *genius*!

MAMMLES: Yes. All those!

ADAM: Better than mine.

MAMMLES: Clouds above your head.

ADAM: Oh neat, Mammles! Try it again.

MAMMLES: Clouds above your head.

(ADAM falls to his knees in mockery.)

ADAM: Oh Mrs God! Mrs God! Make me walk again; heal my
fingers that I may play my violin.

*(MAMMLES is nonplussed. She stares awhile, and then quietly
and kindly...)*

MAMMLES: God is with you, Adam. Listen, and He will be
your music.

ADAM: Oh well. Much to be diddled. Much to be diddled.

(ADAM rises, the loser.)

MAMMLES: Is that Bettya?

ADAM: Bettya?

(ADAM hurries eagerly to peer through the back window.)

MAMMLES: Beside that taffeta Jezebel. At the church gate.

ADAM: *My* Bettya?

MAMMLES: *(Mimics him.)* '*My* Bettya'! – how many Bettyas pass my mirror?

ADAM: Go on, enjoy it!

MAMMLES: She is *not* yours, Adam. Oh, she is not *yours.*

ADAM: Nor was it her reflection, love. Bettya is too ascetic for merry St. Peters. Rough serge and iron pews at Bettya's church. Chapel of Aran or something. They don't say Amen: just baa-a-a-aa.

(ADAM brings an invalid tray, and a silver tray, from the old stairwell R: puts it on the floor, at the foot of MAMMLES' bed RC: then kneels and – from a cupboard at his right hand, sets out an unnecessary array of breakfast cutlery, silver tray, ornate coffee pot, toast rack, sugar bowl...)

MAMMLES: Want me to do my 'up-across and laterals', Adam?

ADAM: There's a splendid Mammles!

MAMMLES: And eat my breakfast every scrap?

ADAM: There's my darlin' Mammles!

MAMMLES: Want my respect and love, Adam?

ADAM: *(Suspiciously.)* Oh yes?

MAMMLES: Marry Bettya, Adam. Go find her. Ask her. *Make her!* I need a woman, a daughter, Adam. Go marry Bettya. She is a good woman. Pure, Adam, pure.

ADAM: Mm, she's dustless and clipped. No hairs below her eyebrows: forbidden, you see. And if by the un-grace of God one sprouted, she'd scrub its shame in meths. She's clean *clean* with scoured pores, and her navel is puttied-over.

(ADAM rams an irritated fork into a bread roll...)

Never heard of beer, hasn't Bettya! Nor spitting, nor armpits. I have tearing urges to scream 'Gee-string' at her music circle; except she wouldn't know what it was – having nowhere to put one.

MAMMLES: Aw, you're past marriage, Adam. Too old. So you blame Bettya. Image transference. *(Nods.)* Image transference. Saw it on television.

(ADAM thrusts the fork-and-bread-roll towards MAMMLES, microphone-wise.)

ADAM: Care to tell the Nation?

(MAMMLES clamps her chin.)

– Go on! – with your belly-sunk bullock-in-septic-tank-God-given voice for here – endething lessons.

(ADAM – still on his knees, swings round and addresses the audience mirror. He holds the bread-roll to his mouth; asummes intimate, cultured, breathy tones; and exaggeratedly moves his head from side to side, following the cue board and keeping his eyes centre.)

After eighty years of touting arrogance and leaping into midsts of ungodlies, Mammles Tanner – from deepest hither-and-thither – now accuses her son of having chapel hatpegs for vital organs.

MAMMLES: You can't make it; and you're blaming Bettya.

ADAM: *(Into 'camera'.)* Thank you; up and out! This is Adam ah – Tanner, returning you to the ah – cardinal's urinal.

(ADAM tosses the bread aside.)

MAMMLES: Nothing but God in Bettya's purity. You were begging for purity a bit since.

ADAM: Purity? *I* was? Was I? Was I heck.

MAMMLES: In your cap'n gown. Grumbling at nakedness and puberty.

ADAM: *Grumbling!* I was *eulogising* it. Oh, move your arms, Mammles. Hup-two: You're chalky, love. Thresh Sunday's blood to your brain. come on! Exercise! *I mean it, Mammles!*

(*ADAM goes to the shelves L for oats, milk, and suchlike.*)

Grumbling! – I sing hossanahs for honest smut and naked children. Oh to be smooth and lithe; every inch of you pure entertainment; to be swinging free in a young world. There's God in nakedness, Mammles; and God in seeing it with a – with a pure eye.

MAMMLES: Your uncle Tobias ordered his parishioners to wear loincloths at the well. But he rescinded the order – spent so long discussing fashions, never got the buckets off their heads.

ADAM: Old beggar missed his excitement.

MAMMLES: What did you mutter, Adam?

ADAM: Mutter Adam? Ach nein!

(*He crosses to the stove R; and prepares porridge in a pan.*)

MAMMLES: You would not have ridiculed me, nor my family, were I free...

ADAM: – And *my* family, surely?

MAMMLES: – The Tanners. Were I free to run down those stairs – to *run*, Adam – would you still ridicule the Tanners?

ADAM: I'd speak my mind, yes.

MAMMLES: Hm. Then rid your mind of evil.

ADAM: *My* mind! Who called those spinsters harlots? Poor little things! I weep for them; clip-clopping to matins, powdered and puffed in mauve; all praying to God the

Curate'll fancy them. And good luck to your twisted Sidesman!

(ADAM lights the gas under the porridge.)

MAMMLES: No luck to him; nor you, Adam. Right name for you, is Adam. Nearly as old as me, *you* are!

ADAM: Give or take thirty years.

MAMMLES: I was young when I had *my* man. *(Nods and cackles.)* You're nearly as old as me!

ADAM: Stoking up, Mammles? All set for a grizzling Sunday? I knew it! –

(ADAM views the packed breakfast tray in satisfaction. He now produces a tiny bottle; Moves to MAMMLES...)

– I knew it when our bellringer's stumbled. Two dongs for a ding, they gave. Always a bad clapper, is that!

(...empties a pill into his hand, and offers it to her.)

Here!

MAMMLES: I'm having no poison.

ADAM: Two mornings you've missed.

MAMMLES: Yes. Poisoning me. You want my bed for a man.

(ADAM bursts into laughter.)

ADAM: Yes, if the week had a diseased crotch, this is it!

(ADAM pops the pill into his own mouth; chews and swallows it with a shudder.)

Urrrgh. Satisfied?

MAMMLES: You palmed it.

ADAM: By Tanner you're a lantern-jawed mountain. All crouched and champing. Chin clamped like a Pre-Raphaelite hinge! Know everything, don't you!

MAMMLES: Yes. I've seen it and been there.

ADAM: Seventy years and never blushed. Chapel ghosts could wag their phallic members and you'd spit unblinking into the font. *(Claps his hands briskly.)* Right! Exercises!

MAMMLES: No! *(Screetches.)* I did them did them did them.

ADAM: Cross your huddle and hope to daddle?

MAMMLES: By the Bible, Adam.

ADAM: Oh, 'tis a puzzle what I should do: I know you're fibbing, Mammles-beloved, you hypochryphal baggage! *(Makes up his mind.)* No! – s'for your own good –

(ADAM reaches his hands towards MAMMLES; she speaks on a near-scream, clutching at excuses...)

MAMMLES: No, Adam, no. That baggage, Adam. Baggage, Adam. Adam, that parcel, Adam...

ADAM: *(Pauses.)* Parcel?

MAMMLES: In the night. I heard rustling, Adam.

ADAM: Rustling? – oh *that's* my scratching at the stomach!

(ADAM hurries to drag a parcel from under his bed DR. It could be a cleaner's box. Its wrapping of brown paper is undisturbed.)

ADAM: – Knew I had an excitement! *(Scratching his diaphragm.)* Oooogh – feathers, feathers!

MAMMLES: Something for Bettya? Adam – ?

ADAM: Mm? No! No no. For Me. A kind of – temporary rib, you might say. Adam's *other* rib!

MAMMLES: I tell you again, Adam; Marry Bettya! Go find her. Ask her. *Make* her! *Adam!*

(ADAM strokes; pats; and fusses the parcel, unheeding.)

ADAM: I'm seeing Bettya tomorrow.

MAMMLES: Fetch the Bible, Adam!

(MAMMLES draws her hand from beneath the sheets. For the first time we see her swollen, gnarled knuckles. And her poor deformed

110

fingers, twisted by arthritis; awesome, mangled things which dangle as carrots from a vile tuber.

MAMMLES can barely raise her arms above sheet level. She points bent-elbowed towards an ancient book on its stand DL.)

Adam! I get headaches shouting.

ADAM: Alright, love. Alright.

(Adam fetches the Bible, hunched under its bulk and weight...)

Ooogh, here's a tonnage of piety! Epistles, d'you fancy, or Gospels?

(...He lays it on the bed.)

MAMMLES: I fancy your hand on the good Book. Your left hand.

ADAM: Touch of the Tanners coming?

(He obeys. MAMMLES lays her crippled hand upon his.)

MAMMLES: Swear by the Lord you will not open your parcel, Adam.

ADAM: D'you think He cares?

MAMMLES: *I* care. Swear by *me* as a mother of the Church.

ADAM: *(Sadly.)* Oh, you're not so pious, Mrs God – Mrs God – not after me and television in this shattered attic. No, there's many a little Adam up your holy jumper, Mammles.

MAMMLES: Not on the Book – !

(She nudges away his hand from the Bible.)

ADAM: – And most of my piety's sunk in your mattress: stifled by flock and physicalities. We've nothing to offer that Book, you and me.

MAMMLES: *(To the ceiling.)* Oh God in heaven! – drop me dead. Send thunder! Take me to angels – if he don't send back that parcel!

ADAM: D'you hear her, God? Eh? Are you coming, Holy Dad?

MAMMLES: In the name of the Almighty, call me to heaven!

(ADAM stares upwards, waiting a moment or so. He wanders to right of the bed.)

ADAM: Nope. Seems you're not going, love. Maybe He heard you fibbing about doing your exercises. *'By the Bible, Adam'!* Eh? Or is He suspicious – that you really don't wish to go?... Tell you what, though – !

(ADAM lays his left hand on the Bible.)

I swear to return my parcel – *providing* – put your hand on mine, love –

(MAMMLES does so; and ADAM places his right hand upon hers.)

MAMMLES: Providing?

ADAM: Providing you open *yours.*

MAMMLES: Mine? I've no parcels.

ADAM: Ah, but you've such a sacred secret box; blue-black, brass-bound –

MAMMLES: – No! *(Drags away her hand.)*

ADAM: Ten minutes, Mammles. That's all I beg. Seven! Five! No – two minutes rummaging, and I'll send back my parcel.

MAMMLES: It's locked, my Box.

ADAM: Key's round your neck.

MAMMLES: No!

(MAMMLES hunches her neck; crosses hands inadequately over her bosom – unable to raise her arms high enough.)

ADAM: It'd snap like cotton, that silly gold chain.

MAMMLES: No! Mine! You respect that Box, Adam. I've earned secrets. Lived for them. Died for them.

ADAM: So have I, Mammles. So have I died.

(ADAM pushes the Bible further down the bed, then places the invalid tray with its ornate silver on the bed before his crippled Mother. The moment is held – whilst MAMMLES sits helplessly, blankly, twiddling her sad useless fingers.)

Wonder what you were up to Out There?
Wonder what you did?

(He moves behind her, speaking over the bamboo bed-head into MAMMLES' ear.)

Many a Tobias missionary must've leapt into clearings, Cross aloft and disturbed a naked rumba. Many a Tobias must have joined in! Eh, Mammles? Did *you* descend to evisceration? Were you disgusting with a pygmy? – Tempted by drumming frenzy, lusting beneath the hibiscus. Oh, what tantalising secrets.

(ADAM moves DL; kneels beside the Box.)

MAMMLES: You will not open that Box.

ADAM: No. S'funny, y'know. I daren't: I'm terrified it's empty. Terrified I'm not His Illegitimate Majesty the Son of Kings: just Dirty Adam out of Wheeltapper back of the sidings. I'd be so disappointed. Button'd boots. Corsets. Dust. Mothballs. Childish scars. An old lady creaking in reverse. Broken potty – 'wicked child!' Fragments of psalter ripped in petulance 'wicked child!'. Are you rambling, Mammles?

MAMMLES: No I'm not, by Christ: and don't ever think it!

ADAM: 'By Christ' from a grizzled Euphemist? Where are the vapours, the helas-helas, the upthrown palms?

(The stove spits! ADAM rushes to stir his Porridge.)

Look at your dread folded arms! If only you'd exercise, instead of fibbing.

MAMMLES: I *did* exercise this morning – a teeny biddle.

ADAM: 1 don't mean a couple of ineffectual flutters like butterflies at poop noddy! Up across and lateral, I mean.

(He demonstrates vigorously – whilst stirring the porridge –)

– Up across and lateral. Up across and lateral. Thresh that blood. Thresh that blood. Up across and lateral.

MAMMLES: Spend your energy on Bettya; we might have a woman round the place.

ADAM: Her serene hygiene, the virgin Bettya! She of the scoured pores. The clean *clean* Bettya!

MAMMLES: Hardly expect sparkling wine with shepherd's pie.

ADAM: Oh, shepherd's pie, am I; I see.

(ADAM turns out the gas; comes to the bedside L.; and empties porridge into MAMMLES' silver bowl, scraping the pan with his wooden spoon.)

MAMMLES: It's too hot.

ADAM: I know.

MAMMLES: You forgot sugar.

ADAM: I did not. – There! Pure cream is that!

MAMMLES: You may leave me.

ADAM: Service, Madam.

(He bows; returns his saucepan to the sink left.

And during the following dialogue, ADAM arranges a curtain above MAMMLES. It is a simple invention of his own: two metal or wooden arms, perhaps, which slot into holes bored in the bedhead...)

ADAM: – And what'd you do, Mammles? Assuming we trundle you into a front pew. Afterwards, I mean?

(MAMMLES is surprised: as though she had assumed her life would remain unaltered.)

Coming back here, are you, love?

MAMMLES: Ah – I ah – I have several plans. Several.

ADAM: Oh yes? Mm?

MAMMLES: I might travel.

ADAM: Travel, eh? Oh. Mm. That'll be joddle!

MAMMLES: And I'd stay in select hotels. Among gentle
    intellectuals.

ADAM: Aha. Be able to manage, you reckon?

MAMMLES: They'd have a lift.

ADAM: Oh! Oh well. Mm.

*(From beneath the bed, ADAM brings a bamboo pole around which
is wrapped old sheeting. He places this pole across the two arms.)*

MAMMLES: Atmospheres of Raffles in Hong Kong. They had
    a lift. And the Royal Amsterdam at Saigon.

ADAM: Oh, we shall Miss you. Bettya and Me.

*(ADAM unrolls the sheeting. It falls, an unfeeling curtain within
inches of MAMMLES' nose. Much of the bed remains visible, and
the shape of her legs, but MAMMLES and her eating habits are
screened from the world.*

*The sheeting is made in two halves, that MAMMLES may hook
them aside if necessary. This she does now. We see her groping
hand – and then her face.)*

MAMMLES: Something been arranged then? Have you
    proposed?

ADAM: It ah – was mutually deliberated.

MAMMLES: Oh. *(She drops the curtain.)*

ADAM: Yes, mutually deliberated; as befitting a piano teacher
    of maturity and a museum curator of shepherd's pie
    standard. We meandered through Keebles auction room
    with long strides, heads nodding. Bettya's arms were
    frontwards in support of her thin bosom; and mine were
    backwards royal-inspection-wise.

(ADAM wanders, head nodding, long strides; arms alternately behind his back, then 'in support of his bosom'.)

– I'm uncertain whether we covered carnality; only logicality and the loneliness of two bachelors.

(He collects a chair DR; brings it UL beside MAMMLES' bed.)

It'd be a dry marriage, I suspect. Sort of 'Kiss-me-Hardy' without navel engagement. *(He sits.)* Doubt if I'd be privileged to view her body much; and if I did, it'd be um – Christmas mandarin behind an April sofa. Yes – a little scrumpled leathery tangerine, it'd be. All right in there, Mammles?

MAMMLES: Yes.

ADAM: On the other hand, she might pant into marriage; twisting and threshing, screaming obsceneties. And me – humdrum Adam, yearning for the sports page.

(MAMMLES hooks aside the curtain momentarily.)

MAMMLES: Suck it and see, Adam!

ADAM: Oh, there's conditions, conditions; hurdles and conditions.

MAMMLES: You'll never marry. *I know you. (Drops the curtain.)*

ADAM: No-o-ogh! All you know is the mask I sneak from our doorknocker coming in, love... Nothing's withered *my* urges, y'know. I'm forever aware of *my* loins. Especially of late. I move through sensations thigh-high. A spiralling prickle to the belly. Odd business at my age. I'm terrified it *is* my age: a desperate storming before the everlasting calm, goddelpus!

(Adam rises; returns the Bible to its stand Down Left.)

I can understand men who – who show themselves to women on trains or in parks. *And I'm not one of them!* Are you listening? Mammles!

MAMMLES: Yes. Yes.

ADAM: Don't want you up nights, deep currents swirling and slopping. Nasty notions bouncing inwards, to be splashed in my face come Easter. Listening?

MAMMLES: Yes yes. Yes.

ADAM: All of us must – must function one way or another, until we're past it. I stagger-by on deep breathing and hard labour. Even so, I've a yearning to – to cry 'Look at me, I'm naked!' Before it's too late – . There aren't so many silk-*loined* years.

(ADAM moves to the sink. There is a hand-basin, already filled with water. ADAM brings it D.C.; places it on the floor in front of his chair. As he does so... MAMMLES hooks aside the curtain.)

What is it?

MAMMLES: Not watching are you?

ADAM: Oh please!

MAMMLES: How do I know?

ADAM: I have not, do not, and shall not watch. He she or it shall not watch Mrs God eating!

(ADAM sits in his chair and MAMMLES lowers the curtain. Shortly afterwards we hear a clatter of overturned silver.)

– What're you up to, Mammles?

MAMMLES: Mind your business.

(ADAM examines his hands; prods his knuckles.)

ADAM: I sometimes imagine *my* knuckles are – .
Little twinges and – . Quite touchy this one! Might be chilblains. I'll need to hurry, but oh for a secret warm girl who smiles and nudges and touches me. The sweetness, the sheer human naturalness of saying – to someone who cares, I mean – 'Look at me, I'm naked!'

(ADAM bunches his fists; presses them into his stomach, leaning forward on a whispered groan.)

Too late for a warm secret girl. And Bettya would never dream of panting nor threshing. So – so it's Adam the ugly ogre, befouling crimpless linen with his bestial urges. She'll reprimand me over a fried-egg-looking boiled. A life of thin furnishings and ever-so-Swedish cutlery.

(From behind her curtains, MAMMLES clang-clang-clang-clangs a spoon against the coffee pot. It is the 'finished' signal.

ADAM rises. He removes the pole and, loosely gathering the sheet, rests it against the wall U.L.

MAMMLES is bolt upright: imperious.)

MAMMLES: I will have coffee in the lounge.

ADAM: Thank you, Madam.

(ADAM takes the silver breakfast tray; places it on the floor. He puts the basin of water on the invalid table.

MAMMLES surreptitiously eyes her clothing and surrounding bedding, seeking traces of spilled food. It is quite good this morning!)

Yes! Very good, love. Just the merest nothing on your pillow.

(ADAM tucks her pillow under his chin; shuffles off the slip. He dips one end in the bowl of water. And he dabs at MAMMLES' hands, her lips...)

Could dispense with Church today, if you like.

MAMMLES: I do not like.

ADAM: Exercises straight after Confession, mind! – if we do have Church.

MAMMLES: No, Adam, no! After the Hymn. It's longer to wait.

ADAM: But I hate doing it, Mammles. Hate doing it.

MAMMLES: We've missed not a single repentance, not one since my Calcification.

ADAM: Oh, I dunno – I'm tired of your knee-deep heathens
shrieking 'I believe' in the Ganges.

*(ADAM wrings out the pillow-slip; then dries MAMMLES' hands
with the other end.)*

– What of poor besotteds who are drowning, like me?
Eh? Over-godded, I am. Over-bombed. Over-America'd.
Over-Spaced. Over-Russia'd. Over-ridden by yelping
self-ignited martyrs. Sodden to my fetlocks in be-damns
and graces until Jesus could descend in hysterics and
He'd be one more putty ball to thwack on a dulled mind.

*(ADAM throws the soiled pillow-slip to a careless corner of the
room D. R. Then he takes the bowl D. L.; empties it into the sink.)*

Yes! – we relish life for fear of God; relish God for fear of
death. Yes! 1 like that. Relish life for love of God; relish
God for fear of death. Yes – *(He returns to MAMMLES.)*
– except I'm over-relished, as well. *(ADAM looks at
MAMMLES, but her eyes are fixed on her mirror.)* Well, Mrs
God?

*(But MAMMLES is not listening. She squints towards her mirror;
and speaks very slowly, stretching a finger to her mouth – a dead
thing, plucking her lip.)*

MAMMLES: I wonder – I wonder what is beyond my mirror?
What sort of new places? Wonder if they are pretty?

ADAM: Were you listening to me?

MAMMLES: No.

(ADAM strides to the door U. L. opens it and shouts...)

ADAM: I'm over-relished as well! *(Slams shut the door.)*

MAMMLES: Adam! Now you have shifted my mirror.
Clumsy bison!

*(MAMMLES glares at her mirror; then her expression lightens,
and in surprise...)*

Oh-h-h-h, I never noticed that before! And a poodle is sniffing the cemetery flowers. *There* is a dismal conclusion to life!

ADAM: I'll swap you, Mammles.

(He returns the chair to DR.)

Your brain, your winter, your death – for my future. Swap, will you? I'm easy.

MAMMLES: So am I.

(ADAM nods, then turns to her, surprised.)

ADAM: Pardon? 'So am I'?

MAMMLES: I need a smoke, Adam. A smoke.

ADAM: *(Moving UR.)* Happy to take your son's life? Is this maternal and proper?

MAMMLES: We are only persons. Two out of a trillion persons.

ADAM: Mutual blood, though. A Tannersworth, at least. I mean, you're supposed to like your mother, and your mother is supposed to – well – !

MAMMLES: I'll have my smoke now.

ADAM: Say you like me.

MAMMLES: I like you.

ADAM: Use my name.

MAMMLES: I do.

ADAM: Now, though. Say 'I like you, Adam'.

MAMMLES: I like you, Adam.

ADAM: And how about 'I *love* you, Adam'? *(He moves closer.)* '*I love you, Adam*'.

(But MAMMLES clamps her mouth... ADAM laughs; shakes his head, covering his face with one hand. He slides away this hand.)

Yes. I'm too close to His holy works. Backstage at
Communion Brewery. Foreman at the Candle Factory,
skimping wax to give less blessed light for a shilling. Or
under the altar, peeping at hairs up the parson's nose.

*(ADAM places MAMMLES' invalid tray beneath the bed; then he
picks up her breakfast tray from the floor and takes it into the
'kitchen' R.)*

MAMMLES: *(Making amends.)* Wasn't too bad.

ADAM: Bad?

MAMMLES: Porridge. Not too bad.

ADAM: There's a crippling compliment for both of us.

*(ADAM brings stepladders from the 'kitchen' R and sets them beside
MAMMLES' bed UR; then he crosses to the wardrobe and dons a
clerical grey jacket.)*

I'm ah – a little peeved, you'll understand. Still – I
suppose we're all sinners. Me, forever falling by the
bedside; and thou, who not only passes-by your son but
kicks him in the gutter!

MAMMLES: You are strange in your ways, Adam. Peculiar.

ADAM: – And dismissed, like those blue spinsters, that
Sidesman, and all other reflections in your back-to-front
world.

*(He takes up a stance; tucks a Prayer Book professionally into his
ribs; and prepares to 'leave the vestry'.*

*ADAM la-la-lahs 'Yes Jesus Loves Me'. And MAMMLES la-la-lahs
in unison.*

*ADAM walks in parsonic atmosphere towards the step-ladders.
And atop them he places down his hymnal, then takes spectacles
from a pocket.)*

T'would seem the choirmaster's organ is short on wind.

MAMMLES: If you're so clever, it should be electric. They have
electric organs.

ADAM: Who – electricians? *(Sings psalm-wise.)* Heaven
preserve my chalky mum from double meanings.

*(ADAM surveys his 'congregation'; he leans his clasped hands across
the ladder-top. His sermon has sincerity; believability. He could
have been a parson.)*

They say the Sidesman is homosexual. Yet I have never
seen him advertise nor wallow puffily. And there are
ordinary mortals who pretend to a spot of harmony
when chatting with musicians. And our Sidesman plays
champion rugger, you know! He will lighten his outlook,
or deepen his voice to oblige. And he's worshipped
by pale blue spinsters of our Parish – by the babies he
chuck-chucks – and the nephews to whom he gives a
purest half-crown.

(Removes his spectacles.)

So, apart from Mammles Tanner who has never met
him, who says our Sidesman is peculiar?

(Pause.)

The sophisticates do! – those whose mouths are
permanently shaped for opening bazaars, who say 'awf'
with the satisfaction of an orgasm, whose bank managers-
my-dear are always 'awf'ly cross with naughty me!'
Deliciously rampant awf'ly cross Mr Such-and-Suches
who tower, blacking out God, through every grinding
conversation: *Sophisticates*! – who are frog-eye'd at ten,
bored by elevenses; pie-eye'd at seven. Sophisticates,
who are forever *awf* on sketching weekends at country
homes of other terribly-terriblies, yet live in dark flatlets
behind Knightsbridge and seldom know where their
next Campari is coming from. Sophisticates who carry
binocular cases with Pan-American labels, containing
two ounces of Saturday cheese from the supermarket.
Sophisticates! – who sew Harris into their tweeds; who
disappear out of Season, trusting we shall assume they
are in Cannes instead of with relatives at Bognor; who

cram their hearts and bellies with cocktail party peanuts; who cry themselves to sleep and *wonder why.*

(Pause.)

They say our Sidesman is peculiar! – and Mammles Tanner who has never met him.

(ADAM gazes upwards.)

And now – do we confess our sins in this humble, miserable place.

(ADAM looks at MAMMLES; she crosses gnarled hands on her lap; turns her face upwards, eyes closed.)

ADAM: I have been peevish with my mother; lacking in respect and my lips are stained with vulgarity.

MAMMLES: I was nouty and would not take my pills.

ADAM: I had ten cigarettes yesterday, and had sworn myself to four.

MAMMLES: I need to smoke. I *need* to smoke, oh God!

ADAM: *(To her.)* And bless you for it! What else have you? Your God is not besotted. Every Sunday you clutter Confession with this smoking pathos. I've told you, dammit, smoke! Smoke! He loves it; so do I.

MAMMLES: You said 'dam' at service.

ADAM: Thank you for your generosity.

(They resume their eyes-upwards attitude.)

I said 'Dam' at Service. And – and – and have greeded in my heart; and envied others.

MAMMLES: I cursed them for being straight and well.

ADAM: *Who*, Mammles?

MAMMLES: Everybody in my mirror.

ADAM: *(Thunders at her.)* You maligned and faulted them for revenge.

MAMMLES: I confess. I confess.

ADAM: *(To heaven again.)* I told a lie at the Museum. And shall try not to do so again.

MAMMLES: I shall try to say – to say 'love' instead of 'like'.

ADAM: Amen!

MAMMLES: *(Quickly.)* And I grumbled over luncheon on Wednesday.

ADAM: And the rest!

MAMMLES: Thursday, Friday and Saturday.

ADAM: Oh Lord – or Nature – Whoever You are: I've mis-used your work. I was given magic and abused it. This mind, these hands. I had greatness in me, and instead am nothing. That's all, I think for today. I'm just a failure, and I'm sorry.

MAMMLES: And same for me. Amen.

ADAM: Amen be damned, you inpenitent pariah! Confess!

MAMMLES: I did.

ADAM: What of your Box, and its shadows?

MAMMLES: He knows, He knows!

ADAM: Who am I? Who was Daddles? My father, who was he?

MAMMLES: Dead. He's dead, Adam. Dead.

ADAM: Not me! – tell God!

MAMMLES: He knows. He knows. He knows.

(MAMMLES hunches, head down. Eyes screwed tight.)

ADAM: Oh well. *(Mumbles professionally.)* Glory be to the Father and to the Son and to the Holy Ghost As it was in the beginning Is now and ever shall be World without end Amen. *(Brightly.)* 'Yes Jesus Loves Me' on Go!

(ADAM replaces his spectacles, end of his nose. And MAMMLES takes a deep breath.)

Ready, Steady. Go!

MAMMLES: *(Together.)* Jesus loves me! this I know,
For the Bible tells me so;
Little ones to Him belong;
They are weak, but He is strong.

ADAM: Are you listening, Martyrs? We're coming! We're coming!

(ADAM descends from the ladders, conducting lustily.)

MAMMLES: *(Together.)* Yes! Jesus loves me:

ADAM: Yes! Jesus loves me!
Yes! Jesus loves me!
Yes! Jesus loves me!
The Bible tells me so.

(ADAM is taking off his jacket. He throws it on a chair. Rolls up his pyjama sleeves; and moves unobtrusively behind the bedhead...)

ADAM: Us, Mammles! Yes Jesus loves *Us*! Belt it out, love!

Yes Jesus loves Us
Yes Jesus loves Us
Yes Jesus loves Us
The Bible tells *Us* so.

(... And on 'so', ADAM grasps MAMMLES' arms. He pulls them high above her head.

MAMMLES drags the last hymn note to a screech of pain. She continues shrieking and shouting as ADAM exercises her muscles.

Round and round ADAM pumps her arms; and he roars to the tune of 'Jesus Loves Me'.)

Up across then lateral,
Up across then lateral,
Up across then lateral,
The Bible tells *Us* so.

(Gradually MAMMLES quietens as her joints loosen. At last, ADAM stands back; moves round to bedside MAMMLES.)

By yourself, Mammles. Don't lose ground. Up across, now! Come along.

(Grunting; worn by effort; MAMMLES bravely exercises.)

MAMMLES/ADAM: *(Together.)* Up across then lateral,
Up across then lateral,
Up across then lateral,
The Bible tells *U*s so.

(During the final chorus, ADAM goes up for a glass of water; brings it back. Then he produces a pill from the bottle and – on the last note – pops it into MAMMLES' mouth.

She is too exhausted for protest.

He gives her a sip of water...)

ADAM: Magnifiddle, love! Magnifiddle, magnifartus, magnunctus dunk!

(MAMMLES swallows the pill with a gulp.)

All diddled and fiddled? And ready for Amen?

(MAMMLES nods. Then, in harmony, they sing an orchestrated AMEN.)

MAMMLES/ADAM: *(Together.)* Ah-ah-ah-ah-ah-ahmen.

ADAM: Pillow slip!

(ADAM replaces the step-ladders R; then drags a large polythene bag to RC. He empties a mass of clothing – presumably fresh from a laundromat, to the floor. And he squats beside it; and roots among it; and ponders...)

I've ah – I've to be earlier in the mornings, from tomorrow.

MAMMLES: Oh? Oh? Shuffling at the Museum, is there?

ADAM: Hello! Pills and porridge, you're deaf; but a sniff of tragedy and up she poddles! Up she poddles!

MAMMLES: Have you been demoted, Adam? At the Museum?

ADAM: Oogh, I'd love a graph of your processes! You know
those electrodes, wired to levers? – I bet you'd signal
stars! Silvered flashings; strange smells of purple; and the
moving pens'd shiver as humming birds. They're um –
shifting me downstairs.

MAMMLES: Nice climax after thirty years of nothing!

ADAM: I am ah – quite a bit upset. Money's the same, though.
And we've had a splurge of redundancy, you know.
Shows they're fond of me, really; keeping me on at all.
Only – you have to go in earlier, and wear a brown
overall.

MAMMLES: Is that in your parcel, your brown overall?

ADAM: No, it isn't, thank you.

MAMMLES: What species of giant wears an overall.

ADAM: Oh give over, Mammles. Often I wore a white one.
You – they wear white upstairs. I mean – doesn't prove
I've failed or – ; but brown is so humdrum. And I shan't
be encountering the general public. Used to like that.
I mean, who goes downstairs! – except to the cafe. But
the cafe is west; and I shall be east. Yes, I suppose I am a
little upset. Never mind!

*(ADAM rises, having found a pillow slip. This he lays on
MAMMLES' bed, and peers at it.)*

Well, your fresh pillow-slip's a-waiting! No holes. No
splits or stains. *(Pause.)* ... no excitement. *(Sighs.)* Monday
tomorrow.

(ADAM stretches upwards with his arms.)

Why is it always Monday tomorrow? A lifetime of
Monday-Tomorrows! A one in seven chance of the
same tatty omen. Why shouldn't it be Muddlesbum
tomorrow? And – Eavensake today!

(ADAM prances behind the bed, forcing a joviality for his Mother's entertainment...)

Hello, Mrs Evans! Going to Chapel on Eavensake? 'Ow's your 'usband? No! There's a posh for you! Startin' work on Muddlesbum, is he!

(ADAM slaps his fist; strides the room, excited with his idea. Yet there is desperation in his voice; tears in his eyes.)

Mammles! – we shall enjoy a different Monday, you and I. In our little world, it is Muddlesbum tomorrow! Furthermore, we shall create a whole new glistening week: Eavensake, Muddlesbum, Tittypot, Widdlytum, Throttlegut and ah –

MAMMLES: *(Growls.)* Fryingpan.

(ADAM winces at MAMMLES' banality; he tight-closes his eyes ...)

Fryingpan! Magnifiddle! This then and henceforth shall be our human calendar: Eavensake, Muddlesbum, Tittypot, Widdlytum, Throttlegut, Fryingpan and Sodemall! Now let's have your pillow, love –

(He tucks MAMMLES' pillow under his chin, and shuffles on the clean slip.)

ADAM: There! And being Eavensake, I'll treat myself to a pair of clean socks, I reckon!

(ADAM squats beside the clothing pile; and slumps, panting and puffing.)

Phew! I – phew – damned if I'm not whacked: threshing blood and tending Mammles!

MAMMLES: I've suffered torments for you, Adam.

ADAM: At my blessed arrival? Are you on at that?

MAMMLES: Torn from my womb, you were. Torn.

ADAM: I am sorry. Try not to dwell on it, love.

MAMMLES: All women suffer. Conception to birth.

ADAM: As far as men know. Monopoly though, isn't it!

MAMMLES: It is God's Will.

ADAM: Mm, but no man'd tolerate it. Don't say I've no clean socks. Um, – proves God's a woman, I reckon.

MAMMLES: Your great uncle said God was a woman. Your great uncle Tobias.

ADAM: Yes. I had heard.

MAMMLES: Tobias believed men revert to women after death. 'Why else have they nipples?' was his theory.

ADAM: Very triddle. Very triddle indiddle. Oh look – !

(ADAM crawls to the bed; reaches beneath; and tugs out a batch of clothing. Shirt. Tie. Underpants. Socks. Handkerchieves. He separates the socks.)

Dear dear! I never washed 'em.

(He throws the clothing towards the dirty pillow-slip D.R. and he sniffs the socks...)

Oh, another couple of days in these.

(He crouches on the floor, struggling into the soiled socks. And he indicates his attic surroundings...)

When I'm through decorating I'll dazzle up the Attic. Haven't scrubbed our alma mater in, oh – many a Muddlesbum, I reckon.

MAMMLES: His wife was the strong one.

ADAM: Uncle Tobias's?

MAMMLES: *(Nods.)* Great Aunt Leah. A real woman, she was. Daughter of a Flemish protestant, was Leah.

ADAM: Yes. She hung above Grandfather's fireplace. Yellow hair round a brow of thunder, like Hiawatha in aspic; clamped mouth scuttering up her nostrils. She permeated that little kitchen, I remember; and glowered through my childhood.

(MAMMLES edges forward slightly; peers crossly over the bed's edge at ADAM.)

MAMMLES: Adam!

ADAM: Mm?

MAMMLES: Adam!

ADAM: I heard you. I heard you.

(ADAM screws his neck to look up at her; and they are clamped eye-to-eye...)

MAMMLES: These are *my* memories. *You* have no claim to history.

ADAM: Mm, deep deep jelly behind those eyes. *(He turns back to his socks.)* Keep talking, love. You may recall something important.

MAMMLES: I remember Vauxhall Gardens. Little girl, I was. Leah on the harmonium, and Uncle Tobias rising to preach. 'On the third day –' , he shouted, '*She* rose again'. And ten thousand people rioted.

ADAM: Only used to be five hundred.

MAMMLES: Tobias was martyred in the Crimea.

ADAM: Thus ended another Tanner.

MAMMLES: He was martyred, Adam. Captured by the enemy; scourged and stripped. Snow to the ankles; but they immersed him in a barrel of vinegar; and taunted, as he spoke of God. Twenty-three hours, until he sank beneath the brew. A diving dwarf retrieved him. Your great uncle was puckered as an ox's stomach; skin tanned to potash. But he died with Jesus –

ADAM: – According to St. Mark. I know. 'And they gave Him a sponge of vinegar; and He did drink'. And I know how it tasted.

MAMMLES: *He* was a real man. A *real* man, was Tobias.

ADAM: Ah – till he took up his nipples after death, o' course.

(ADAM puts on his shoes again; rises; and moves U.L., stamping his feet.)

By heck, these are corrugated!

MAMMLES: Your great aunt Leah was eaten in New Guinea. Not from anger: rather as a token of reverence. She was deserving of heaven; so they ate her flesh, and pickled portions of her body to make the Tribes holy.

ADAM: Yes. Show me a bottle of chutney – I'm away.

(ADAM plugs in the electric kettle U.L.)

MAMMLES: Respect for your betters, Adam! You'll have less call to peddle your failures at confession. Leah was a Saint.

ADAM: *She* was a saint; *he* was a man; and always at Humdrum Adam's expiddle! You, your holy aunts and jungles! Your Jesus-Wars, your suffering and fighting! Always made me so inadequate. Bravest thing I ever did was put out a fire in my inkwell.

(ADAM moves to a cupboard above the sink; brings out two tea-mugs.)

MAMMLES: *(Calls.)* Nothing to stop you rolling your sleeves! Look at this home! *My* home. Filth and smell! I was reared in majesty; graciousness and sweeping banisters –

ADAM: Oh She-above! She-above! Forgive Mrs God!

(ADAM moves to the bed; puts the mugs on the bedside table, L.)

MAMMLES: I was sweet and attractive: they queued for my name on their cards.

ADAM: Want to see your photo, Mammles? *(Points to a drawer.)* Shall I fetch her? – that thumping, steaming wench of lantern jaw and piano legs? Lucky you married Christ, Mammles! You'd've got no one else.

MAMMLES: I was handsome.

ADAM: Ah! – *handsome. Handsome* I'll give you.

(ADAM crosses to MAMMLES. She turns aside her head; but he whispers close to her ear.)

Who crept away because you weren't handsome *enough*, Mammles? Eh? India, wasn't it! – I've checked dates. Son of a yak-driver, am I? Kiss your feet beneath his chariot wheels, did he, then rush for purdah? Tell me, love! *(Shouts.)* Tell me! – if I'm deserving, I'll thrust a ruby in my nostril, and double on zittar. Here – !

(ADAM hurries behind the bed to the other side. Again MAMMLES turns aside her head; again he whispers close.)

– Or was it back of the sidings over the Heap; Grandfather spitting wrath on your carnal horrors, and cursing you to Madras with your squeaking bundle! *Who am I? Where was it?* In the *gracious* scullery of Grandfather's *sweeping* railway cottage, your majesty?

(ADAM crosses back behind the bed to the shelves DL. He reaches down a biscuit tin.)

Remember! – if I'm an humdrum flunkey, you're an humdrum flunkey's mummy, love! Curious how exotic grows your history, the nearer you come to stagnation. Furbishing ancestors with snippets of late-late show; giving Leah to cannibals!

MAMMLES: Leah was eaten, Adam. She was eaten by an unfriendly back pew element.

ADAM: 'Unfriendly back pew element'! What's this? Political witticism?

(ADAM takes two teabags out of the tin; returns the tin to the shelves.)

– Leah died in a home for gentlefolk. I visited her. Forgotten, hadn't you, love!

MAMMLES: Um – political witticism? – um –

ADAM: I visited Leah, Mammles. But her mind was bubbling, and her legs'd collapsed – like yours, love. Cannibals hate lisle-skinned water-logged knees, you know.

(ADAM puts a teabag into each of the mugs.)

Twenty-three years on crumpled hunkers, was Leah. And her only talent was reciting the Gospels in Swahili. She was cracked, dirty fawn, forgotten, and lost – all through having no loving son to cherish her! How about that, Mammles!

(No answer.)

I'm waiting for reactions, Mrs God-Tanner! Sorrows. Regrets. Apologies!

(ADAM strides to the front door; flings it open.)

(Shouts.) Mammles Tanner's a wretched liar! –

MAMMLES: You are sickening, Adam!

ADAM: – *(Shouts.)* Hear all about it! Are you down there, Homosexual Sidesman?

(The kettle is boiling!

ADAM slams the door. He moves D.L. , unplugs the kettle, takes it to the bedside, and pours hot water into the tea mugs.

He adds milk. Then he takes MAMMLES' invalid tray from beneath her bed, and sets it in place. Next, he snatches a clean shirt from the laundry pile DR, and moves UL, putting it on. – And he roughly irons it by stretching and tugging it –

Suddenly he pauses; glares at MAMMLES...)

I am waiting for an apology – !

MAMMLES: I had eight brothers, missionaries. Five sisters, nuns. Four uncles, nine aunts, and my father, all in the service of God.

ADAM: Is this an apology?

MAMMLES: I've known pain, Adam. I battled with suffering and sickness. I nurtured the weak and visited lepers –

(ADAM moves swiftly to her side; whispers close to her ear.)

ADAM: Ah – but you were robbed of martyrdom, love! No crucifixion! Upside down like St. Peter'd've been nice. *Oooogh, lovely that*! But no! Fancy having to rot in peace with Humdrum Adam whose bravest deed was putting out a fire in his inkwell! Right – !

(ADAM moves below the bed to the wardrobe DR; grabs a black tie from within it.)

– You glory in your ancestors; and me in the Admiral!

MAMMLES: *(Anxiously.)* Adam! No, Adam!

ADAM: Excitement day today, love. Excitement Eavensake! A re-birthday for humdrum Adam.

MAMMLES: One of my relatives was eaten, I remember. Perhaps uncle Tobias was eaten –

ADAM: – Great Uncle Tobias! Symbolic mother of Man; sister of She-God. Now where is that Empire News of 1935 – ?

(ADAM stands on a chair to reach the wardrobe top and rummages among piled newspapers and books, tossing them to left and right.)

They're demanding his committal. The Editors. All in black and smudged-white. *Where is it*! Blotch on England, my great uncle. Claimed he was pregnant at seventy-three! Notorious at maternity hospitals. Appeared on saints' days demanding admittance.

MAMMLES: Cheap denigration. Tobias was martyred. He was martyred, Adam, in a barrel of vinegar.

(But ADAM has found the newspaper. He drops it on the bed before MAMMLES.)

ADAM: *(Quietly.)* Great Uncle Tobias died in a circus. Page ten. Column two.

(MAMMLES sweeps the newspaper from her bed to the floor.)

– He crouched in a glass cage, wearing lipstick, pompadour wig, and singing 'Unto Us a Child Is Born'.

Sixpence to go in. They billed him as 'This Happy Hermaphrodite'. Tanner for a Tanner. And a guinea for guessing what sex he was!

(Now! – with reverence, ADAM produces an Admiral's jacket from the wardrobe. Gold braid. Chestful of 'fruit salad'. Glorious. Next follows an Admiral's cap. Scrambled egg. ADAM wears the cap, and crosses to the 'audience mirror' whilst donning the jacket. He views his appearance. All he needs is a battleship. ADAM looks magnificent!)

MAMMLES: Not the hat, Adam! The hat is not required.

(ADAM backs from the mirror. He picks up his mug of tea at MAMMLES' bedside UL; then sips, considering himself appreciatively.)

Adam! *The hat is not required.*

ADAM: Oh, I was bound to trespass one day.

MAMMLES: You will not leave this room!

ADAM: But I must. I must. To see if I make sense.

(Replacing his mug of tea, ADAM searches for sunglasses; finds them above the sink somewhere.)

MAMMLES: Sense? Kissing yourself in mirrors? – because you're scared of kissing Bettya?

ADAM: I'm ah – fond of Bettya. Bitterness creeps and scuffles now and then, but I'm quite fond of her, really. Except – *(He stops.)*

MAMMLES: Except what?

ADAM: *(Shrugs.)* Things.

MAMMLES: Things are anything. What sort of things?

ADAM: Conditions.

MAMMLES: See *me* grovelling for conditions! Bring her! I'll dictate to Bettya. I'm the Church Elder. Bring her to face *me*!

ADAM: She can't bear your hands.

(ADAM dons his dark glasses, as though to hide his eyes; and unable even to face MAMMLES, he speaks to the mirror.)

Your hands turn her stotmach. Gets crawling inside, she says, to even imagine entering this 'sordid place'. She marvels at how I exist with such a nighttnare; wonders why I don't dispatch you to a home. And *that* is the condition.

MAMMLES: For ah – for marriage?

ADAM: *(Nods.)* Her serene hygiene is stiff; tight; dry and clean. She abhors anything loose, damp and *rancid.* It would be kinder in a Home, she says. You'd be happier in a Home, she says.

(ADAM swings to face MAMMLES.)

Well, you asked me! And – *(Removing his dark glasses.)* – I've told you.

(Their eyes meet. Then MAMMLES stretches her hands towards him, slowly – though not as a plea for mercy; not in humility; but in impulsive gesture of disbelief! She would draw ADAM closer if she could, to bring his eyes to her own.

Suddenly, ADAM crumbles; falls to his knees; clasps his hands in his lap.

And it is so incongruous, this crumpled 'glorious' Admiral!)

Oh, why wasn't it different? Couldn't He or She have granted you a moderate, nice martyrdom? A swift idolater's knife; or sucked to heaven through a warmish swamp! ... I could've been so great. My intellect – above average, you know; my brain; my painting; my poems. I *should've* been great. Only – only I haven't the action, d'you see, Mammles. Know what a genius would've done? A genius? He'd've skewered you to the bedpost, love: soon as your legs failed. Pointless, a legless missionary, see! So he'd've executed you, Mammles.

(He nods to himself.)

You'd've gone happy; and I'd've proved my dedication. *If* I'd been a genius. Only I know I'm not. And it's crucifying us both.

MAMMLES: Yes –Yes –

(She begins to shiver…)

You've opened my mind to f-fear. I'd planned on a woman c-com-comp-companion. Now I'm getting nothing. N-nothing. Not even a c -crumpled Admiral!

ADAM: Sorry. Sorry. *Sorry*. SORRY!

(ADAM scrambles to his feet.)

MAMMLES: When do we need to answer this condition?

ADAM: Tomorrow. After tiffin.

MAMMLES: Tiffin on Muddlesbum.

ADAM: Aye-aye, love. Now – !

(Briskly, ADAM sets a candle-in-a-bowl-of-water – obviously a standard arrangement – on MAMMLES' table. He lights it. Then he puts a tub of cigarettes beside it.)

– no boo-boos, Mammles. Pluck with your mouth; and no singeing your hair, or taking up thy bed to walk. And see –

(ADAM brings a serviette-shrouded object from beneath the bed; places it on MAMMLES' pillow.)

– it's handy and tiddly. No toppling over. Did it once upon a tiddle, remember! So be warned. Alright.

(ADAM strides to the door L.)

MAMMLES: Go on, Stifflegs! See who needs you!

ADAM: As you will. Kiss the Captain's arse and all who sail in her!

(He salutes and Exits.

MAMMLES grips the mug of tea between her wrists, and conveys it to her mouth. But before sipping, she laboriously checks to ensure nobody is peeping at her crippled eating habits. MAMMLES sips; and sighs; and blinks; and thinks.

Now, MAMMLES lifts the cigarette tub between her wrists; plucks a cigarette with her lips: and lights up from the candle.

Again she peeps clumsily about her. And she puffs; and blinks; and thinks.

Outside, faintly, the Salvation Army Band strikes up: "Jesus loves me! this I know". And MAMMLES strains for a glimpse in her mirror. Obviously, the Band is streets away; yet still she stretches and hitches and grunts. Then she sags back, defeated.

She takes the cigarette from her lips, trapping it between her index knuckles...)

MAMMLES: *(Sings.)*   Yes Jesus Loves us
         Yes Jesus Loves us –

(She stops dead; sets her face stubbornly; and alters the last word.)

         – *me.*

(And with evil satisfaction, concludes the hymn lustiy.)

         Yes Jesus Loves *me.*
         The Bible tells *me* so.

CURTAIN

ACT TWO

The Admiral's uniform on its hanger is hooked over the water tank DL.

ADAM is painting inside the front door. He has white-emulsioned the background, and currently adds green wavy stripes.

U. L. the chest of drawers has been similarly painted; the paint pots stand beside it; and ADAM makes constant trips back and forth replenishing the brush. In turn, he adds a green stripe to the table and door.

A pause.

ADAM considers his efforts, leaning an appreciative head this way and that.

MAMMLES is dozing through evening church bells; a clatter of imperfect changes. Ding dong Di-ding Di-ding di-dong.

ADAM's eye is caught by the water tank DL. Taking his green paint pot, he creeps over; brings his uniform to MAMMLES' bed; then paints waves on the tank... and bubbles... and a fish with popping eyes.

And he is much pleased by his artistic labours!

ADAM re-charges his brush, and surveys the room for other worthy subjects. His eyes fall upon dozing MAMMLES!... He sneaks close to her, the brush raised – no, better not! ADAM returns upstage L. to the front door.

The Bells ding-dong to a sudden stop. And MAMMLES awakens at the silence. She stretches her shoulders, grunting.

MAMMLES: Why is my mind busy? What is my tick-tick-ticking?

(MAMMLES squints towards her mirror...)

Closing in, the evenings. They've lit the lichen light. See the stragglers! Nothing *but* stragglers. Aw, my father! – He'd lived and lusted; braved God and the lash. His belly was muscled, his chest deep and strong. But this lot! – they've no meat, no spunk for catching your eyes.

ADAM: Back in the land, are we? Back in the lubber?

(MAMMLES eases her head around; tries to peer upstage at ADAM...)

MAMMLES: Oh, now I know the tick-ticking. *You're* back!

ADAM: Back! I've been back; cooked your lunch; emulsioned my background; and started my wavy lines.

MAMMLES: What did we have?

ADAM: What did we have what?

MAMMLES: For lunch.

ADAM: Bubble and squabble. And you scoffed every morsel – between glowers.

MAMMLES: Gave me heartburn.

ADAM: Gave you a nice snoozle, too!

MAMMLES: Forty waddles, no more.

ADAM: Forty waddles! It's dark! My emulsion's dry, and I've started my wavy lines. See!

MAMMLES: Mmm –

(Mammles views the new artwork...)

– and how tawdry *between* your lines! 'Tis your mind you're painting, Adam; *(She nods at the Dragon.)* your darkness crawling out.

ADAM: I'm decorating your back-to-front world, Mammles. Ooogh, you're an evil besom, on the quiddle.

(ADAM puts his paint pots and brush in the sink.)

I almost decorated *you*, during your thousand waddles. Wish I had now.

(MAMMLES leans forward; thrusts ADAM's uniform from the bed to the floor.)

Hey – !

(ADAM hurries round; picks up the uniform; dusts it; and hooks it on the dragon wardrobe, downstage end.)

This is rented; has to be returned un-damaged.

MAMMLES: You can keep your clown's moteley off *my* bed.

ADAM: Now! To the Oracle!

(He consults a list pinned to the back wall.)

And we shall consider our duties for this Eavensake evening. Ah – I did your spirit rub Widdletum, was it?

MAMMLES: *(After thought.)* Fryingpan.

ADAM: No, it's Pensions Fryingpan: must have been Widdletum. Now – um, how about toenails? Tackle those, shall we?

MAMMLES: Feet are ugly. Old handbags mouldering. Ugly.

ADAM: All the same, we'll have a diddle. Scissors, um –

(ADAM searches for scissors.)

MAMMLES: Most things I've done; but never bowed my head to feet. Show me a sufferer. I'll name his sin: gout for greed, pride for bunions. Devil stalks, they are. God popped our stomachs to hide them.

ADAM: Oh, I dunno. *(Points at the Bible.)* Didn't one of your chaps rush about washing people's? Ah! –

(He finds the scissors in a shoe!)

Knew I'd put them somewhere safe. Now then – !

MAMMLES: No! No! Stop!

(As ADAM perseveres, dislodging the bottom blankets, uncovering MAMMLES' feet, she rocks frantically and screams on a prolonged note.)

No! Cease! Sto-o-o-o-op!

ADAM: *(Stops; forced patience.)* The nails will grow inwards. Into your flesh, Mammles. They *need* cutting. It's a *need.*

MAMMLES: I should vomit to touch a person's feet. I despise you.

ADAM: Right! *(Clapping his hands, brightly.)* So, who d'you fancy – the postman? Or how about Smoothie-Tight-Lips, your holy Doctor, with his bedside crinkles? I can see *him* doing it! Which only leaves your homosexual Sidesman.

(ADAM strides to the door; flings it open, and shouts...)

Hey! Homosexual Sidesman! Fancy trimming my mater's fawny-beige horny toenails?

MAMMLES: Exhibitionist!

ADAM: No, sssh! *(Shouts.)* Homosexual Sidesman! Are you there, love!

MAMMLES: 'Tis *your* disgrace. They never see *me*.

ADAM: Listen! Delighted, he says. *(Shouts.)* You shall have tea and seed cake afterwards: never notice the clippings!

(ADAM slams shut the door; leans his head against it; then twists wearily, his back to the door.)

'You'll need do everything', he said. '*Everything*, Mr Tanner'. He was firm, throat-clearing, and brief. *(Clears his throat in imitation.)* 'Everything, I fear!' He had the gravity of one who is returning to Milady on her lawn; and the twins tumbling flushed from Harrow.

(ADAM rushes his hands to his face, speaking into them; eyes hidden.)

And every Sunday I hear them growing. Creaking, skewering, scratching my mind.

(He sighs into his hands breathily; uncovers his face.)

Give over fighting, Mammles! Look on it as a kind of atonement like I do.

(It takes several seconds for ADAM to regain brightness. He deep breathes; exhales; then slaps his fists.)

Away we go!

(ADAM sits on the bed, alongside MAMMLES' ancient feet. He begins clipping. MAMMLES turns aside her eyes, tight-closed; and her head, as far as she is able.)

ADAM: Oh, they're not so baddles! Bit jagged. Have you been biting 'em?

(For a while, ADAM clips in silence. And then...)

I always remember a little girl – You never visited me at Welsh Auntie's, did you? I'd be fourteen, I reckon. No, you were reassuring lepers at Zamumbotti or someplace.

MAMMLES: Meerhut. I had the Mission at Meerhut.

ADAM: So when were you reassuring lepers at Zamumbotti, then? Mm?

(No answer.)

Suppose it was between taking Christ to New Guinea, and clothing the Naked of Chile.

MAMMLES: Your Holy Aunt Cora was martyred in Chile. Ambushed by river tribes. Cut her throat; and gave her to the fish. But not until eight of them'd had their pleasure.

ADAM: They say shrimps have fun, too.

(ADAM moves to the other side of the bed; and the other foot. Clip, clip.)

Anyhow, this little Welsh girl – oh and I did so love her. I loved her so much. Glowing; and crisp; with a kind of Alice-in-Wonderland bottom. Swooping, curving rearwards; and me, stammering crimson. And um, we were in the Barn. I forget how. 'Feel my heart thumpin'', she said; and squeezed my hand over her little left breast. But I noticed her finger-nails bitten to the quick. Put me right off! Still – I did so love her –

(He pauses wistfully.)

– and her Alice-in-Wonderland bottom.

(He rises; brushes clippings to the floor, and tucks in the sheets. Then he looks at MAMMLES. Between her teeth, humiliated and bitter, she rasps...)

MAMMLES: *Thank you.*

(ADAM scrapes clippings under the bed, using his toe.)

ADAM: I'll sweep those later.

(He replaces the scissors, then consults the list UL.)

Mm. Supper at seven. Washing up. Then we're clear, I reckon.

(...he stands square, facing the list, scratching his behind. Then he turns briskly.)

Yes. Except for – ! *(Exercises.)*

MAMMLES: *(Brightly.)* Turn on television, Adam!

ADAM: There's only God until seven-twenty-five. You always curse television-God. No spunk, you say.

MAMMLES: Ah no. No, turn Him on, Adam.

ADAM: I hadn't forgotten Exercise, love.

(MAMMLES swivels her eyes to him, disappointed.)

Every morning, lunchtime and evening. Up, across and down to the lateral. Every morning, lunchtime and evening.

MAMMLES: *(Hoarsely whispers.)* You're killing me, Adam.

ADAM: No-o-ogh. *I could've made you walk.* One spot o'faith, one syllable of encouragement, I could've been great; *and made you walk.*

MAMMLES: *(Whispers, close to tears.)* I'm finished, Adam. Leave me solid. Leave me solid. Watch television.

ADAM: *No!* Television *after* exercise. Whilst I am caring, you will keep moving. Maybe you *should* pray for a Rest Home. They'd leave you solid there. By hell, they would!

(He Moves DR; takes a hanky from the clean laundry; returns the rest of the clothing into its polythene bag, then tosses it out of sight. And glumly...)

Oh, I wish we could find a woman for the ironing. Laundromat tomorrow. *(Sadly.)* Muddlesbum tomorrow.

MAMMLES: No children, Adam.

ADAM: Mm?

MAMMLES: No children.

ADAM: No children? Children what? Me no children?

MAMMLES: She's at the change, your Bet – your woman.

ADAM: She is?

MAMMLES: Must be at her age. Besides, you say she is too clean for *that.* I suppose you'll sit in Archeology using your brains.

ADAM: Mammles, um – *(To behind the bed.)* – I was disloyal, criticising Bettya. I mean, she's not that bad. Isn't sensuous; isn't young; but – oh so awful you should use *my* words against her.

MAMMLES: You said them.

ADAM: For fighting back, though... Seventeen years of Mrs-God-Tanner between cycling to the Museum; we're married, love! You and me are married! So when a lover – quotation muckles – comes on the scene; and Bettya does have a faint, irritating superiority; and – well, you fight back. See? *But she's not that bad.*

MAMMLES: She's bad enough.

ADAM: 'Enough'! Enough doesn't apply at my age. At my age 'dreadful' would be marvellous.

MAMMLES: You don't have to grovel for it.

ADAM: Oh, you're talking through your insulted hands. Who's grovelling? Alright, alright. *I am*! I am grovelling.

I um – I didn't intend, you know, this morning, telling what Bettya had said.

MAMMLES: We shall not mention her name.

ADAM: Mustn't blame her too much. Bettya had two –

MAMMLES: – *We shall not mention her name*!

ADAM: I'm only saying Bettya had two old folk –

MAMMLES: *Do not mention her* –

ADAM: *(Topping her.)* – *She had two old folk of her own*! I won't be silenced! 'Excitement Eavensake' Mammles! Remember! There'll be changes. Bettya nursed her parents for most of her dry life; can hardly expect her to start again.

MAMMLES: And where are they?

ADAM: I don't know. Dead.

MAMMLES: Mm. She buries them, and begins work on me!

ADAM: – Only to your greater glory, Mammles. Nobody is antagonistic: desperate yes! – but for a solution to *your* comfort.

MAMMLES: Oh yes? Oh yes? Aha. If you please – !

(MAMMLES points an imperious hand towards the Bible.)

In parts of the East when death is near, they deposit their elders in a hut outside the village.

ADAM: Really? I thought orientals worshipped the aged. Where d'you want?

MAMMLES: St. Matthew.

ADAM: Aha, I thought so!

MAMMLES: Oriental elders are so obliging. They wither to nothing, wagging their minds behind them; and die unsurprised like – frogs.

ADAM: St. Matthew 26. How's that for you? *(Sets the Bible before her.)*

MAMMLES: I was twenty-six. A laughing doctor took me to see them; maybe – oh I can't say how many poor dying ancients on wooden tiers. They blinked at me; weakly; faded. And beside each was untouched rice, water, and a waiting shroud delivered by the least important daughter.

(MAMMLES licks her wrist; flicks over a Bible page.)

We returned over the Kwantock Bridge. The Doctor held my slim waist; guided my pale, tapering fingers. I remember thinking 'Thank the Lord I'm young, with a long long while to live'... But I'm here now.

ADAM: Here is everywhere, Mammles. And far from China.

(He moves to Left of MAMMLES.)

MAMMLES: Mm.

ADAM: I um – enquired at the Eltham while I was out.

MAMMLES: *(Reads.)* 'And forthwith he came to Jesus ... and kissed Him'.

ADAM: Fancied a hotel, you said. This morning.

MAMMLES: *(Reads.)* 'Before the cock crow, thou shalt deny me thrice'.

ADAM: Aw – can't we discuss what's to be diddled?

MAMMLES: Too much has been duddled.

ADAM: Marvellous at the Eltham. Tiddly matriarchs tripping to high tea in blue rinses. Private bathrooms. 'Oh delighted! delighted! one lower-front vacant!', they said. Perfect for an admiral's mother.

MAMMLES: Oh, even went *there* in your shame.

ADAM: We-ell, they don't know me. Shan't be returning, anyhow. It's thirty eight guineas; excluding newspapers and fruit juice. Thirty eight guineas! Didn't tell them you were crippled. God, what an extra!

(He tests the paint on one of his decorated pieces of furniture. It is still wet! So he moves DL for a turps rag to clean his fingers.)

147

Oh, what's to be diddled, Mammles? I've had no rest in weeks. Counting patterns on a three o'clock ceiling; thud thud thud. Fitful aching on a crushed ear. Oh to press a button and drop you into sunny pink in the something-or-other home somewhere.

MAMMLES: Is something preventing you?

ADAM: Love and respect. And the dread of waiting – because there *is* no quick button.

MAMMLES: *And* the thirty eight guineas, Adam. And the thirty eight guineas.

ADAM: That as well, yes. But mainly the preparation; consultation; documentation. Sign this; swear to that. Two carbon copies of your blemishes. How's your father? *Who was he?* Insurance cards. Do you solemnly swear you're destitute? Ever had VD? Stick a tick in the box! Bad breath? Stick a tick in the box. How old are you? *How old are you?* They'll ask how old *I* am!

(ADAM crosses DR He drops the turps rag on to the Dirty Pile; chooses a soiled garment, and rubs his hands dry.)

I'm old enough to be married and have grandchildren.

MAMMLES: No need for questions, Adam. Telephone the Poor House. Say a redundant human's awaiting collection.

ADAM: But there's a queue for growing old.

MAMMLES: Say I'm alone and helpless. Telephone 'em, Adam! Go on! Then hide in the park saluting sailors.

ADAM: God – !

(ADAM slaps his fist, groaning with frustration; then he swallows his anger; and returns the Bible to its stand, crouching on his haunches DL beside it.)

And ah, who am I supposed to be on this telephone?

MAMMLES: A son who died. You are dead to me, Adam.

ADAM: Not to them though. They'd poke and priddle: under the bed; into your Box. Oh, they'd peep in *there*, you know! Who irons your bodice, they'd ask?

MAMMLES: Who nailed Jesus to the Cross?

ADAM: Ah, but you're not answering subsection 592 on form 38. See, love? *They've* no dotted lines for the Father, Son and Holy Ghost. God only gets a hoot in triplicate.

(MAMMLES holds out her fearsome, knotted hands.)

MAMMLES: *(Shouts.)* Then tell 'em I am tired of living. I'm ugly – obsolete – and I want to die.

(A pause.)

ADAM: *(Quietly.)* Wish you weren't so cruel to yourself; and me.

(ADAM, still crouched DL, nods towards MAMMLES' Box.)

All these years, and I've never seen inside. Amazing restriddle, I reckon. Remarkable will-puddle. Any ah – any money in there, is there?

(MAMMLES stares at him a moment.)

MAMMLES: There're no pieces of silver.

ADAM: I j-just – just wondered.

(ADAM goes to the sink; washes his hands.)

Anyhow, destitution is out. Not allowed, unless you're stinking in a hovel, covered in lice. Show them a couple o' savings certificates, a bow window, and a dead son who makes your tea; they'll bleed you white, love!

(Whilst ADAM is drying his hands, MAMMLES licks her wrist; flicks over a few Bible pages.)

MAMMLES: Did you ever – *(She pauses.)*

ADAM: Mm?

MAMMLES: Look at me, Adam? Let me see your eyes.

ADAM: Eyes what? *(He moves UL to face her.)*

MAMMLES: Did you ever know a woman, Adam? None of your Welsh children. A woman, I mean.

ADAM: I knew Miss Renshaw from Welfare. Oh – you mean 'know' as the Bible has it.

MAMMLES: I mean as a *man* has it. Did you have carnal knowledge of this Miss Renshaw? *That* is what I am asking.

ADAM: Ah, Inquisition, is it!

(After the style of a Court Usher, Adam shouts his name – fading his voice down distant 'corridors' –.)

Calling Adam Tanner!... Adam Tanner!... Adam Tanner!...

(He crosses the room left to right, heavily, as a prisoner from deep cells.)

Clang!... clump clump clump clump clump clump... Clang!

(ADAM enters the old stairwell R, hands on the railings like an Accused in the dock.)

Do I swear to tell the truth, whole truth, and nothing? So help!... I do... Name? Adam Tanner. Caucasian. 160 lbs. Last seen with his mother's victuals, present and passed. Age? *(Shouts.) Who cares! Why do you always ask my age!* Sex? Male – apparently surprisingly. Occupation? An almost-was. Father? Unnecessary. Question: did you know Miss Renshaw. Did you? *DID YOU: ANSWER!* ... Um, may I use my own words, Mrs God? Oh, certainly, my son. We are here to help you, Child.

MAMMLES: *(Nods.)* Yes. 'Tis all between your wavy lines.

ADAM: We met in Ornithology behind Case Nine. Miss Renshaw was younger than my serene hygiene the virgin Bettya.

MAMMLES: In her thirties, Adam! Your latest one's old; Renshaw was old; all your titty friends are old.

ADAM: *(Hotly.)* Renshaw wore a veil in Ornithology.

MAMMLES: She was old! *Admit it*!

ADAM: *(Nods sadly.)* She came to me from her dressing table, thriving on prayers; heart double-thumping. Explosions of powder, encrusted where tactless crows were treading. You had to peep past that veil; crumpet in gossamer with spasmodic dots. *(To MAMMLES.)* Those sprinkled dots on veils – can you position them for strategy? *No matter. Keep to the subject, Adam Tanner! Right*!... Blue eyes; anxious lids. And big white teeth, the front ones pricking her bottom lip. Tiny puckers at her chin, like a linen-imprinted elbow. Pucker pucker pucker...

(ADAM comes out of the 'dock' to RC.)

...Could be a mother image, I suppose... and you know the Museum flagstones? Her footfall was un-precise; made me cringe. We hate looseness, Mrs God! ... Into the Jungle, knees back; Tight buttocks and Bible aloft; *Lick my boots in the house of the Lord*!... Click clack click slither click slither click clack slither slurge click clack. 'Hello. Am I frightfully awfully late, Adam?' 'No, that's alright'.

MAMMLES: There's a rash of obscenity.

(ADAM sits on the bed (R of MAMMLES).)

ADAM: *(Smiles.)* Yes, I'll give you that, Mrs God... And there was a cinema. Marble vestibule. Click clack click slither click slither click clack. I felt old in the upper circle. Unnecesary among children. The film, cold and foreign. Ingar Ingar thwank and thump. Iron stairs and hollow clunks; echoing corridors; boys in tassels. The later Miss Renshaw was coarse at the cafe. She stuttered over sexual words, her mind bruised, spongy, from creating opportunities for saying them.

MAMMLES: As close as you ever came, Adam!

ADAM: Nope! Oh no no no, Mrs God!

(He swings round, and backs triumphantly into the 'dock' again.)

Nope! I submit to Mrs God that we met in Hadley Woods on an August Fourth. Well – ? Mm – ?

(MAMMLES narrows her eyes; stares at him; says nothing.)

Question! – how many times, how many times, how many times? We'll see! Question: was this the end? No. She asked me to marry her back in Ornithology behind Case Nine ... Green paint bubbles on the window ledge. I popped them with my thumb nail, and made tiny hot cross buns on the way back.

(ADAM prods his thumb along the 'dock railings'; then back again.)

'Why don't we – Ha-ha – get married, Adam?' ... A shutter over my mind. Words frozen. Tick-tock shouted a clock; and Filby in far-off-Fossils shouted 'No touching!' at someone ... She turned her back. Trembling creases in her dress. Middle-aged jowls flushing red. Mottled legs, through hugging her bedsitter fire. Tick-tock thundered the clock. '*No touching: No touching*!' ...

(ADAM walks his fingers along the railings, and fades his voice as Miss Renshaw's 'footsteps' recede into the distance.)

... Click clack slither clack click slither click slither click clack click clack click clack.

(He comes out of the 'dock' and – in sad bewilderment, asks MAMMLES.)

Wonder why I gave up slippers by the fire? Miss Renshaw wasn't all that bad. Nice little lady, on the quiddle.

MAMMLES: You never said if ah – if ah – if in Hadley Woods, ah – ?

ADAM: *(Brightly.)* Well I'll tell you: we shall prepare a Brief. On one side you write my father's name and how many times you took over me. Then I'll happily oblige on the other!

(ADAM claps his hands, and points to a clock.)

Oh, quarter to sickle!

(He fusses towards a tiny bottle on the bedside table L.)

MAMMLES: Aw, stop faffing your pills!

ADAM: Eye drops, love. Eye-drops.

MAMMLES: Oh.

(MAMMLES lowers her jaw, squints upwards, stretching open her eyes.)

My mother's eyes!

(He unscrews the dropper from the tiny bottle; measures a dose.)

Banking on the mother image, aren't you!

It was not me who said it.

(ADAM administers the drops into MAMMLES' left eye. And MAMMLES blinks the liquid under and around her lids.)

ADAM: I evolved with women, as a little lad, through a forever of washdays, Varicose veins, scrubbing boards, steam and grunts; blubber-festooned haunches and walloping bosoms. 'Him' was their common enemy. Not me, I mean – another 'him'. *Him* and what he did in bed. *Him* with his phlegm and fags and belching. *Him* and his trousers – *trousers!* – vile double-bagged things, peeling their skins to offend the pit of a lady's stomach. Right eye, now –

(ADAM moves round the bed to R, measuring another dose for MAMMLES.)

– And after squelching their dismal little 'hims' to beggary, guess who was thrust to glory! *You*, love! Mrs God! 'How's your dear brave mamma', they asked, 'that wonderful wonderful woman fighting for the Lord in those nasty jungles?'

MAMMLES: Jealous?

ADAM: Not then.

(He puts drops into MAMMLES' right eye. As before, MAMMLES rolls the liquid about her eye.)

MAMMLES: Now.

ADAM: Perhaps.

(ADAM returns the eyedrops to the bedside table L.)

MAMMLES: Finding a psychology for monkhood, Adam? *Monkhood?*

ADAM: I'm no monk, love! –

(ADAM sits on the step DR, considering his Parcel ...)

At least – not yet. No, I'm wondering if a mother image is plausible – for a quasi-orphan. Hardly ever saw you as a toddler. I remember peering skywards at a blistering suntan, dangling crucifix, and the piercing eyes of Mrs God. 'This is your mummy, Adam'. *It is??* Oh, I remember that Box –

(And he crawls like a child towards the Box.)

– smelling of camphor and pepper. Aunties rushing; taxi honking, grandad roaring. (I) remember a quiet moment by the open lid, tracing my father's face in acorns and leaves. Didn't ever change it, did you? The wallpaper lining?

MAMMLES: Didn't I?

ADAM: Well, I thought I could see my father's face in the leaves. Then great aunt Abigail slammed the lid.

(ADAM rises; moves UL.)

MAMMLES: I detested Abigail. She whipped me. Abigail. And dragged me to Father.

ADAM: Oh? What for?

MAMMLES: (I) detested Abigail. Glad when she was martyred. And she *was* martyred, Adam. In New Guinea. She *was*.

ADAM: I know. I know. I'll give you Abigail.

MAMMLES: Stretched beside her torn Bible. Genesis in one ear; Exodus in the other. And no trace of Leviticus or Numbers.

(MAMMLES beings to laugh...)

No trace of Leviticus or Numbers!

(... she falls into hysterics of mirth. Adam joins in; and wipes the tears from her eyes.)

Oh yes. Oh yes. Yes, I hated her portrait on father's mantel.

ADAM: That was Leah, love. Great aunt Abigail hung over the chiffonier, looking like Nero in a diving bell. Confusing for a child: couldn't understand how my great aunt became Emperor.

MAMMLES: They kicked her out of Westminster Abbey. Ah, you were a man in those days if you wore knickerbockers. She refused to remove her hat; so they kicked her out.

(More laughter.)

ADAM: I can remember a voice – in my cradle, this! – a man's voice saying Abigail Tanner is so holy the sun shines from her bottom.

MAMMLES: Oh that was Abigail. Yes. Yes. And no trace of Leviticus and Numbers --!

(MAMMLES is away again! So is ADAM.)

ADAM: I spent my springing years watching Abigail's bustle; and never saw the light.

(More laughter together.)

MAMMLES: – Nor Leviticus or Numbers!

(Hysterics together! ADAM moves B.C., laughing. He quietens; folds his arms on the bedhead, and speaks over the top at MAMMLES.)

It was a comfortable voice – in my cradle. Warm; and exuding blessed disrespect for the holy Tanners. Was it my father's voice?

(MAMMLES does not answer.)

Was it my dread unmentionable DaddIes?

MAMMLES: Perhaps you –

(She pauses, and tries to fall into laughter again. But the mood has changed.)

ADAM: Yes, love?

MAMMLES: – Perhaps you are seeking a father image, and Bettya is a man.

ADAM: Aha. I see. And for such bitter remarks I intend marrying her. She is a little piece of twisted string. So am 1. And we shall be honourably, um – knotted.

(ADAM drags an old Ewbank from the Stairwell R; and sweeps the areas left and right of the bed.)

MAMMLES: Decided then!

ADAM: Decided! Don't fret, though: I'll settle you somewhere nice.

MAMMLES: *(Mardly)* Don't want strangers mauling me in the Poor House.

ADAM: I do understand. You want Mary Poppins and we can't afford.

(From now on, the dialogue is speedy and brittle.)

MAMMLES: A real wife'd share your obligations.

ADAM: Bettya has clearly defined limits. She is healthy, frigid, available for reasonable partnerships, able to drive; and does not undertake scivvying.

MAMMLES: Perfect wife!

ADAM: This morning I was homosexual because I wouldn't have her; tonight I'm twisted for needing her!

MAMMLES: White wedding, of course.

ADAM: Of course.

MAMMLES: And ah –

ADAM: – Yes? *(Then louder.)* Yes?

MAMMLES: Shall you be piped aboard?

(ADAM hurls the Ewbank into a corner, and storms to his own bed.)

ADAM: I shall bequeath my wardrobe to the Vicar!

(He bundles the Admiral's uniform into the wardrobe.)

MAMMLES: And your Parcel?

ADAM: My Parcel –

(He throws his Parcel into the Wardrobe, too.)

– can go to hell tomorrow.

MAMMLES: Out of sight and settled!

ADAM: Out of sight and settled.

MAMMLES: You will be nothing without me.

ADAM: Oh! – the all-holy Tanner of Tanners, only begotten mother of mothers! So sacred, I wonder I have a navel.

(ADAM slumps on to his bed.)

Ever noticed my morbid navel fetish? It's through having Mrs God for a mother. I contemplate myself in panic, lest I discover a bereft belly – and my umbillicus rising midst angels to the East.

(He rises, imitating wings with his hands. And he crosses Left.)

I'll tell you something, love! *(He pats the Bible D.R.)* You'll find Adam in the Bible. I'm there. *But where are you?*

(He moves UL.)

Nobody is anything without someone. Like everybody else, I thrive on reflections. No existence without reflections. I'm um – I'm an illusion, an unnecessary mind until I register on someone else.

MAMMLES: Mm, well without me you'll have nothing but mirrors.

ADAM: *(Irritated.)* Without *anyone*. Yes. That's what I'm saying. Yes. Yes. Yes. Without someone, or you; or Bettya. Yes!

MAMMLES: Oh? Does she agree to ah – does she even *know* of your games at mirrors?

(ADAM is becoming more and more heated. He indicates the 'audience mirror'.)

ADAM: This mirror – there's no crime, no madness in this mirror. You, me, or anyone, exist only as *we think* other people *think of us*!

No such animal as a real person, love! Not you; not me! We're not real -- except in our own tiny minds, according to our own insgnifficle measurement of thought! ... So don't multiply my doubts please! I've enough wretched doubts without you breathing on 'em.

(ADAM faces the mirror.)

Nothing unusual in there. *(He nods at the 'mirror'.)* It's a harmless 'let's pretend'; nice, effective people I yearn to be. My kind of preacher; my kind of teacher; my kind of *someone* – if only I had the ability to walk out and *be* that someone. Which I haven't!

MAMMLES: The Admiral walked out.

ADAM: He was a minor psychosis, saluted by one policeman *once*!.

MAMMLES: He walked outside, Adam. He was a lie, and a madness.

ADAM: *(Hotly.)* I created the Admiral for *you*! That's how he
started! So I could people your calcified attic with funny
faces and hope and sermons on Sunday. By Goddles! –
you fight cruel-and-bitterly.

(ADAM moves behind the bed to R.)

So wicked to malign my mind and body for your own
gain!

(He swings round accusingly.)

And how do you know I shan't have children? Maybe I
might have children. I don't know how old Bettya is – not
really; nor how cold. And I was most capable with Miss
Renshaw, thank you! I'm happy to say I managed um –
sportingly well in Hadley Woods.

(ADAM is telling the truth.)

(*Very quietly.*) And with a lady called Joan – one short
evening; and little Phyllis in Wales.

MAMMLES: Oh? Have you just – ?

*(MAMMLES sways slightly, eyes flickering upwards. A momentary
spasm.)*

ADAM: What is it? What is it?

MAMMLES: – Nothing. Have you just remembered your
sporting record?

ADAM: No, I – I betrayed a tiny proud secret or two; and now
I despise myself for bragging. Always been so faithful to
my ladies.

(ADAM lifts MAMMLES' mirror off the hatstand; looks into it.)

I am a braggard in face of mirrors. It helps me. Helps
everyone. Even you, Mrs God.

MAMMLES: *That*! You may smash *that*, Adam. 'Tis nothing to
me.

ADAM: And destroy your daylight; your fourth wall; your
passing world?

MAMMLES: They're only real people out there. You *can* smash *real people*. It's no loss.

(ADAM holds the mirror closer, closer to MAMMLES' face. She turns aside her head.)

ADAM: Sidesman, lichen gate – all gone; and no Blue Harlots to curse and confound. You'd be nothing! Because it helps – shouting at mirrors, doesn't it, love!

MAMMLES: I don't reach anyone back there.

ADAM: What if you couldn't *see* them, either?

(MAMMLES pushes aside the mirror with her forearm; and coolly, calmly...)

MAMMLES: Smash it, Adam. I told you! ... Smash it, Adam! And with my eyes shut, I'll be closer to real living and dying than you'll *ever* reach! Smash it, Adam! *Smash it!*

(ADAM hurls the mirror into a corner U.R. It shatters. He turns slowly to the railings R; leans a hand against them, shaking his head.)

ADAM: *(Whispers.)* Such a senseless waste. God, I detest you!

MAMMLES: Yes. I was detested at the Mission for denouncing fanatics: holding their eyes to the sun. Detested for crying when girl babies were given to the river; male infants castrated for glorifying temple choirs; children mutilated to enhance their begging cups. Oh yes. Oh yes. I wept for Sanity; and they detested me for *that*, also.

(She twists to look at ADAM, scornfully.)

I am sure you are worshipped at the Museum. Dear suffering Adam – *(In mock aside.)* 'and his crippled mother, you know'. Sweet Adam, kicked downstairs and pleading for more. Brave Adam, beloved by everyone.

ADAM: Everyone? I have never noticed you on my team.

MAMMLES: Ah well you have Bettya. Shall you be grovelling for *her* praise; cutting *her* nails; washing *her* mouth?

ADAM: *(Quietly.)* I know. I know.

(He sighs and moves behind MAMMLES' bed.)

I ought to be sanctified, I reckon. Ought to be a special medal for all unknown persons! – just in case they did a little something – somehow – sometime.

MAMMLES: They gave a priest in Meerut a medal; not until he was dying. My brother Caleb and me watched him die. Nursed him. I dreaded the feeding. Oh, I dreaded the feeding; the working of his mouth. The gristle and click, the moving veins.

(She narrows her eyes in distaste...)

And so ah – ah – so *I* eat behind a curtain. My decision, remember. In *my* ~ home.

ADAM: *(Simply.)* I'm sorry your final chapter is so – inglorious.

(ADAM leans over the bedhead; kisses the top of her hair. And MAMMLES – encouraged, beckons with her clawed hand. ADAM moves round to R of the bed.)

MAMMLES: Adam! Here, Adam! Closer! Look into my eyes, Adam. No – look deep! There is an infant, a child, a nymph, a woman – all in this mind. I am *real*, Adam. Not cardboard for filing; not meat for surrendering to doctors. I live, Adam. *And I live in you.*

(Suddenly ADAM falls to his knees at the bedside.)

ADAM: Oh Mammles, Mammles. Hug me – hug me –

(He pulls MAMMLES' arm about his neck – struggling closer, his knees beneath the bed, his chest against the bed's edge.)

I need love, Mammles. Just some love. I dream of love.

MAMMLES: Cannot imagine *me* dreaming. Different species, me! 'How did *she* – !' This is you, Adam; this is you! 'How did *she* ever lust in young shadows, and sigh for honey!'

ADAM: Put weight in your arm, Mammles. There's no pressure; no force.

MAMMLES: Dream without sleeping, I do. Flunkeys crowd this attic marvelling at my decisions. I run down these stairs, shaking hands with bishops –

ADAM: *(Whispers.) Hug me, Mammles!*

MAMMLES: I had a mind. An intellect. *I could have been great.* But they sent me among priests and unambitious virgins. An uncertain girl, I was. Cursed, *I* was! – for one clumsy little sin. *Well now I'm glad!* Ha!

(She nods to herself.)

MAMMLES: Oh, I dream of my husband –

(ADAM raises his head; looks up at her. MAMMLES is aware of this, but continues – after the slight pause.)

– My husband worships me; strokes me; finds every segment of my body to his satisfaction.

(MAMMLES looks down at ADAM, then draws away her arm from his shoulders.)

Oh yes. They think dreaming shrivels with age. *(She closes her eyes.)*

ADAM: I've considered every kind of husband. Tried all computations. Even considered your brother Caleb. So alone out there, I mean. You and he. I mean –. Only you harp on my mental stability. Well, I mean you *do*, love. So – was Uncle Caleb my father?

MAMMLES: I need my privacy, Adam. My privacy.

ADAM: Oh!

(With moderate haste, ADAM fetches the pole-and-sheet, lodges it in position, and as in Act One, the sheet rolls downwards – an unfeeling cloth wall, until MAMMLES is hidden from view.

ADAM moves behind the curtain and stoops – as though bringing something from beneath the bed. His movements are more an atmosphere, than an observed action. We may guess; but there must be no lavatorial suggestions.

Indeed, there are many reasons why MAMMLES might need privacy: such a helpless ancient human so constantly dependant upon others. To be alone. And secret...

... where nobody can even hear her. And for this added reason, ADAM hurries to put a record on the gramophone D.R.

LAND OF HOPE AND GLORY thunders forth, clicking and scratchy. Well worn.

ADAM folds his arms, and waits. So often he must have waited thus! He glances idly. Shifts position. Considers the ceiling... the walls... the floor.

MAMMLES' Box catches his eye! And he wanders towards it, plucking his lip ... This might be his last opportunity for opening it! Why not? Why not?

With cautious glances towards the curtain, ADAM kneels at the Box. He removes the cover and quietly eases open the two side-catches; but the centre one seems firmly locked.

With his palms on the lid, and his fingers each side the centre lock, he exerts all his strength – trying to squeeze the Box-front inwards (and away from the lid) ... It does not work. ADAM sits on the lid, his back to the bed. He tries the same plan...

... The catch flaps open! And at this exact moment 'Land of Hope and Glory' sticks in the groove. The same phrase is repeated:

Dum De-dah dum. De-dah dum. De-dah dum. De-dah dum.

ADAM rushes across; snatches the pick-up from the record. He is panting. Heart thumping.)

MAMMLES: Adam?

ADAM: Yes?

MAMMLES: You may remove the curtain.

ADAM: Yes, um –.

(ADAM looks at the Box; then at the gramophone. No more need for music. Yet so near –! He decides to take a chance; and replaces the pick-up arm.

'Land of Hope and Glory' continues ...

ADAM goes behind the curtain. As before, he attends to any requirements; then reappears and hurries cautiously to the Box. He kneels, and raises the lid.

There is a top tray filled with neatly folded garments, all black. But ADAM is drawn to that old wallpaper – the same acorns and leaves he remembered.

He traces his finger across the patterns; twists his head this way and that, trying to re-discover his father's face...

...Then the record sticks again!

Dum-de-dah dum. De-dah dum. De-dah dum. De-dah dum –

ADAM freezes; indecisively looks towards the gramophone and above him, MAMMLES' hand is groping at the 'curtain'.

Slowly, painfully, the sheet is hitched aside – and MAMMLES' face appears. ADAM drops the lid and stares up at her.

MAMMLES utters a cry. She tugs at the sheet, trying to raise herself; but the pole collapses across the bed, and MAMMLES falls backwards...

De-dah dum. De-dah dum. De-dah dum. De-dah dum. De –

ADAM rises; throws the pole-and-sheet behind the bed.

Then he hurries D.R. and takes off the record.

There is no going back! So, ADAM drags the Box to ULC...)

ADAM: I want to know, Mammles. Tell me! Or I look for myself.

(He opens up the lid. MAMMLES refuses to look. She stares straight ahead.

ADAM turns to the Box; closes his eyes ...)

Camphor and pepper! And Granda' s kitchen. Schooltime. A thin-ness of pens; the hollow clack of a fallen rule; and that first frightening room you never discover again.

(ADAM opens his eyes; looks at the box; then swings round to MAMMLES.)

Well? Why is it such grinding sacrilege? All in the family, isn't it? – Isn't it!

(But MAMMLES stares ahead, refusing to acknowledge his presence.)

As you waddle, Mrs God! As you waddle –!

(ADAM roughly unpacks the top tray, piling garments on the floor. He brings out three black dresses, various gloves and blouses; high button boots; a parasol; and an ulster cape.

ADAM looks at MAMMLES. No reaction. So he removes the top tray and empties the lower section. He produces a black coat with fox fur collar; a vast crocodile handbag; various black skirts; a feather fan; crocheted shawl; patchwork quilt; and an Indian topee.

He feels around the sides of the trunk. Empty!

ADAM frantically searches the black handbag – which reveals a long-handled ivory shoe-horn; and nothing else.)

Nothing! Nothing! Nothing to tell; nothing to hide!

(ADAM surveys the sad piled clothing at his feet. He rubs his forehead with both hands; then drops his arms in bewilderment, and swings round to MAMMLES.)

Why? *Why?*

MAMMLES: It was mine. My one secret place, free from public inspection. It was my Box.

(ADAM sighs in pity; then hardens himself. He begins throwing clothing back into the Box...)

ADAM: You still have my father. *And* a magnificles moment of martyrdom.

(MAMMLES flops back against the bedhead. Her eyes are closed. She lies still.)

– Real top Tanner! Lips pursed in purity, head at holy tilt; brow of sweet wrinkles; and Lord curse Adam for knowing what he did!

(ADAM replaces the top tray; flings in the rest of the clothing.)

Fifteen years! Fifteen years of tip-toeing reverence and unfulfilment; grunts and creaking shoes. Take care! Take care! Gentle Jesus watching. – And I couldn't even find my father's face.

(ADAM runs his fingers over the wallpaper lining, then slams shut the Box lid.

Suddenly he notices MAMMLES...)

Mammles? ... Mammles? ... Mammles–!

(ADAM puts an arm around his Mother, eases her forwards.

She works her mouth, trying to speak...)

MAMMLES: It was a soldier, Adam. A – a s-soldier.

ADAM: Yes, love. Never mind. Never mind.

(ADAM supports MAMMLES, comforting her.)

MAMLESS: A – a soldier, Adam; so long ago.

ADAM: Oh, Mammles! – to go back *with you*! Marching, fighting, preaching. Oh the throbbing hopeless pain for that lost age! Oh to take your hand, and drag you to life.

(He half rises, holding MAMMLES' shoulders...)

Let's go, Mammles! You and me! I'll be your strength. Come to life, Mammles! Come to life! We'll parade your Bible. Tanners ho! Mrs God and me against all Man's Loneliness! Eh? Eh, Mammles! Eh!

(MAMMLES shakes her head.)

MAMMLES: Only shadows out there. We should – should limp among ruins, pretending.

ADAM: Yes. And we'd need permission to go.

> (*ADAM rises from the bed; fusses MAMMLES' pillow.*)

Lie calm, now. I'll bring help –

> (*He moves a step away towards the door, then turns.*)

Somebody high up, was he? Colonel or a captain?

> (*MAMMLES shakes her head.*)

Lieutenant?

> (*She shakes her head again.*)

-- Sergeant?

MAMMLES: No. It was only Private Smith.

> (*ADAM nods and moves slowly to the door L.*)

ADAM: Private Smith. Not half the fun of wondering; nor the tingle – of Uncle Caleb.

MAMMLES: – Can marry Bettya now.

ADAM: Yes –.

> (*He turns; looks at MAMMLES; then turns back to the door, and leans his forehead against the frame.*)

> (*Whispers.*) I can't marry Bettya for the sake of marrying. Take this woman – for desperation. I want my own special girl – I know there *is* one.

> (*ADAM pulls himself together.*)

I shan't be long. Only a muddle.

> (*He exits. We hear his footsteps descending ...*

> *MAMMLES raises herself slightly, and calls...*)

MAMMLES: Adam! ... *Adam!*

> (*ADAM's footsteps race back up the stairs...*)

ADAM: What? What is it?

MAMMLES: I'm hungry.

(ADAM rushes into the 'kitchen' R, grabs a pan, then races across to the shelves L for oats and milk and ...

... then he stops; and stares incredulously.)

ADAM: Thought you were dying!

MAMMLES: So did I.

ADAM: Oh? Dying of anything serious? *(He moves to the bedside.)* Were you pretending, Mammles? I'd never forgive that!

MAMMLES: Would you not? And was I?

ADAM: Every breath of rebellion, and you'll begin dying! Lolling your eyes like a rearing nag. And I'll never know.

MAMMLES: Know about Bettya, though. Settled *her* – haven't we, Adam.

ADAM: *Were* you pretending?

MAMMLES: Self-righteous Adam! Arrogant Adam! Nothing – without your mummy doll. Mighty in your reflections; brilliant in your dreams; and once past that door – dumb and un-needed.

ADAM: *(Fiercely.)* And you have never been wrong: Very waddle –!

(ADAM drags his parcel from the wardrobe.)

From henceforth I shall be scintillating, reserved, humble, proud, pure and dirty, hateful, loving; not black; not filthy white – and I'll be half way to becoming thoroughly misunderstood.

(He pauses a second, sadly.)

I shall be pawnbroking in space. Plenty of clocks and watches; nobody wanting the time... Happy medium between one and three balls. Two are unforgiveably human.

(ADAM rips open the parcel. He drags forth a monk's habit.

168

He kicks off his shoes; and dons sandals from the parcel; and then a white rope for his waist. Finally, a large wooden cross to hang about his neck...

He admires himself in the audience mirror.)

MAMMLES: Sixpence to see great uncle Tobias in his glass cage. How much to look at you, Adam?

ADAM: How much to look at me? Oh, I should get a season ticket, love. I may be Pope next week.

(He claps his hands briskly. And he nods towards the oven.)

Well! D' you fancy supples fuddle, followed by evensong?

MAMMLES: No. Evensong fuddle; and supples after-waddle.

(ADAM turns to the audience mirror:)

ADAM: We are all in disguise, Children. Siblings-All, are we, in a Life of Lies: all disguised like Mammles-God in her rat-tail wig – wearing my skin for protection; and you Children sprouting hair to hide your doubts.

(He nods.)

I'm from dusty Archeology, half-past Ornithology Case Nine: an intellectual parrot rich in Longest bridges. Ask me! I'll tell you. I'll tell you. I'm easy to find. Easy to find. Look under Weights & Measures left of the Hebrew Calendar.

(He strikes a pose.)

How many maggots stand end to end on a rotting crumpet? Ask me! I'll tell you. How do Lady Peers stand in the House of Lords' Loo? I'll tell you. I'll tell you.

(ADAM crosses to MAMMLES' bedside.)

By Christ, I'm a new Adam. Reborn, I am. I'll be up those stairs at the Museum, a constant ascent to Glory. I shall solve essential mysteries. And as for you, Mammles,

I might even heal your poor tortured hands. From Adam to Adam, Amen.

(ADAM picks up a Mitre-shaped tea cosy.)

ADAM: Are you game for a quick Blessing, oh Mother of Tanners?

(He plumps the tea cosy on his head bishop-wise, raises two hallowed fingers, and in sing-song tones:)

Abber-Tanner-dabber-dee-dah.

(MAMMLES falls into hysterical laughter, rocking helplessly, her crippled hands stabbing the air. ADAM capers around the bed, popping in and out of her view, comically repeating his tea-cosy Blessing. And we realise that a Sunday Ritual has run its course, as it will next Sunday and on every other Sabbath.

The Children are singing again: faintly at first , then louder and louder. "Yes Jesus Loves Us". The lights fade, diminishing into a circle around our two gnomes in their weird little world.)

CURTAIN

STAIRCASE
JUST CHARLIE AND HARRY

J ust *Charlie and Harry,* my two lonely hairdressers in a basement shop.

Impresario Bill Freedman loved *Staircase* and he told Peter Brook. Peter Brook told Peter Hall, and Peter Hall told happy-Me that he was determined to direct *Staircase* for the Royal Shakespeare Company with Paul Scofield as Charlie. But we had Whitehall adversaries!

In the Spring of our England 1966 the Lord Chamberlain ruled as Censor. Hallowed was his name, suspicious his mind and vicious his blue-lead-pencil. And he savaged my *Staircase* script. Out! Outraged, he was. *Why?* Peter Hall appealed, so he and I were summoned to a joust at St James's Palace where Henry Eighth once trod.

We trudged under archways of weeping stone, up tumbledown steps, across groaning oak into an ancient cubby hole. There, in a comfy swivelling chair, a quizzically-staring fellow sat: not the Lord Chamberlain himself, but one of his merry Grumblers – whose smiling Hello shrivelled into an attack on Harry's innocent line:

It's years since I woke up clutching the quilt for shillin's.

"And you wonder, Mr Dyer, why we ban such a speech?"

"Yes I do, Sir. I am bewildered."

"Clutching a *quilt for shillings,* Mr Dyer? Who is paying these shillings?

"Paying – Sir? Nobody. It's about Harry's dream of riches."

"Oh yes, no doubt! But whose riches is he clutching?"

Peter Hall and I were mystified. As a Playwright I am never intent on equivocation or prurience. My explanation was easy:

"Harry feels too old for dreams. In younger times he'd dream of shimmering shillings and, even as he awoke, his treasure still glistened on the eiderdown – there! – inches from his chin. But when he reached from his dream, his fingers clutched nothing but air." (Into which barrel of depravity was the Censor delving?) "What did *you* think I meant, Sir?"

Chamberlain's Man huffed an *oh,* an *um,* and *oh very well.* But he counter-attacked: "And what of these Men hugging and kissing at the first Curtain?"

Peter Hall said it was hardly kissing " – and not that sort of hugging."

"Does your Shakespeare Company, Mr Hall, rejoice in such dialogue as *'Oh, Charlie you poor old bugger'?"*

"We've used worse."

"Not in homosexual context, I trust, Mr Hall." Chamberlain's Man accepted 'beggar'. But the Hugging was out. Out out!

Not so! Peter Hall fought stubbornly on, describing Harry and Charlie as Kafkaesque:

" – two of Life's puzzled victims. Their lonely hearts bleed in secret. Does Mankind not hug a wounded heart? Would any Man not hug a dying friend? Would *you* not hug your frightened brother?"

We kept the hugging.

ALDWYCH THEATRE – NOVEMBER 1966

'Smash hit, we were! The Season opened with *Staircase* in repertoire with several other Plays but gradually, by the New Year, we became the Aldwych Theatre's main presentation.

The RSC even created special twice-nightly performances for *Staircase* at 5pm and 9pm.

Broadway followed. Paris. Berlin. Rome. Everywhere.

Certainly, *Staircase* raised the wind in our British Parliament, with friend and foe harrying the Speaker: 'what foul this, what filth the other, blah-blah'! Subsequently *Staircase* starred throughout twenty-odd pages of the *Joint Committee on Censorship (HM Stationary Office HL255)* and was a major influence in ending the Lord Chamberlain's role in British Theatre.

CLEOPATRA'S TITTY – THE FILM

Stanley *(Singin' In The Rain)* Donen produced and directed my *Staircase* screenplay for Twentieth Century Fox. Richard Burton, an idol of mine, played Harry to Rex Harrison's Charlie. For a clutter of reasons they shot *Staircase* in Paris, France; we filmed at Billancourt Studios along the Banks of the Seine.

At close of a filming day in late 1968, 'front office' sent me to a sound stage – quiet-and-dim save for Donen, Burton and Harrison circled in the beam of a working-light, three mumbling witches finger-stabbing my Shooting Script: the speech where Charlie is cruel over a pimple on Harry's naked head. Charlie says Harry's head looks like Cleopatra's titty.

DONEN: *(With his Southern drawl.)* Cleopatra, Cha-a-arles. Rich and Rex feel we should have someone else's titty.

ME: Oh?

BURTON: We were all in the *Cleopatra* Film, see, Charlie: Rex, Elizabeth and me. Liz played Cleo. People might think my wife's titty is Harry's pimple, see.

ME: Ah!

Elizabeth Taylor and Richard Burton were famously married, and seldom separated. Liz was filming at nearby Boulogne Studios. She threw a Banquet for the Duke and Duchess of Windsor. And I, Charlie – born into sandwiches on a Council estate, I sat at her pretty left hand (a tale for another day). Elizabeth Taylor, she of most beautiful eyes; could there be a lovelier titty?

REX: *(In his high voice)* Some other lady's breast, Charles. More diplomatic.

DONEN: Boadicea, Cha-a-arles, would you go for Boadicea's titty?

ME: Ummm –

BURTON: No, no, no! People call her Bo-dicky. 'A belligerent wench, anyhow. 'Can't have an armour-plated titty for Harry's head."

REX: Flo' Nightingale has a ring. Nicely medical link to the Pimple.

DONEN: Nightingale's titty, Cha-a-arles?

ME: Aha!

BURTON: No! She's too damn clean! How can Harry's head look like a holy woman's titty no one's likely to have seen?

Stanley Donen fell apart: he'd been choking on giggles since Breast One. Richard's boyish grin blossomed into laughter, and I joined in. Even Rex unfolded into a smirk. I forget which lady's bosom prevailed. I shall have to watch the Movie again.

* * *

One aspect of *Staircase* awaits unravelling. Early on, with my Curtain Line barely dry, I submitted *Staircase* to a possible Star who reacted emotionally and accused me of parodying his partner and himself. It was a shock. Fiona and I had trodden the boards with many a Charlie and Harry; never would we have maligned beloved friends. Yet the more I protested the more frantic the Star's obsession which culminated in silly threats. What a to-do! And what to do?

I consulted James Grant Anderson at whose knee I learned the nuts-and-bolts of Theatre, of contracts, box office, and management. He presented tours of my Plays. I co-starred with him. Jimmy-Gee-A had been an actor-manager since elephants were woolly. Noël Coward wrote of him fondly as *Ham-but-pure-York*. Frenetic, shameless, James took curtain-calls hissing *bastards-bastards* through smiling teeth at unresponsive audiences. And Jimmy-Gee-A solved my puzzle in a merry second:

"Easy-peasy! Give Charlie your own surname. You can't sue yourself, laddie."

So! I intertwined myself throughout the *Staircase* duologue, thereby adding a useful extra dimension.

Beginners Please!

* * *

STAIRCASE

Just CHARLIE and HARRY.

Presented by the Royal Shakespeare Company
(in association with Bill Freedman and Charles Kasher)
at London's *Aldwych Theatre* on 2nd November 1966
with Paul Scofield and Patrick Magee.
Directed by Peter Hall.

* * *

Presented by Freedman & Kasher at New York's *Biltmore Theatre* in January 1968 with Eli Wallach and Milo O'Shea.
Directed by Barry Morse.

* * *

La Comédie Des Champs-Élysées presented *Rattle* in Paris, April
1968, with Paul Muerisse and Daniel Ivernel,
directed by Claude Sainval.

* * *

The Play is enacted in a London Barber Shop called *Chez Harry*
during a Sunday night in 1960. The action is more or less
continuous.

* * *

ACT ONE

Customers enter Chez Harry *beneath a staircase leading to rooms above. There are two barber chairs, basins, mirrors, etc, and through windows we see the street and a striped pole. At Curtain Rise, CHARLIE 'suffers' in his chair whilst HARRY shaves him. The latter has a red-embroidered 'Harry' upon the pocket of his white jacket.*

And, strangely, HARRY's head is swathed in bandages!

As he works, HARRY jigs and mouths in time to the Hallelujah Chorus *which thunders from a record-player. After neatening CHARLIE's sideboard with a razor-flourish, HARRY fetches a hot towel from the stockroom. He fusses CHARLIE's face; holds up a mirror, etc.*

Now, HARRY swaps his jacket for a cardigan. He whips the sheet from CHARLIE's chin, wraps it about himself, and sits in his own chair.

CHARLIE rises, dons his own white coat (with red-embroidered 'Charlie'), and turns off the Hallelujah Chorus. *Then he brings another hot towel, plops it upon HARRY's face, and pats awhile:*

CHARLIE: Funny day. Sunday.

> *A pause. CHARLIE sniff-sniffs towards the stock room.*

> That boiler is a herald of death. We need that gas man, that gas man.

HARRY: I don't need him. 'Hate that gas man's hair.

CHARLIE: Oh lovely. What! Each time you open the door, the flame goes puff.

HARRY: All nice and homely, dear.

CHARLIE: Witty, Harry, witty! Let's hope you're still giggling when they find us stiff and carbonised or whatever.

HARRY: Can you do that blackhead by my jawbone?

CHARLIE: Oogh you obscene bag. Where's your culture? Sssssh!

HARRY: What?

CHARLIE: There she goes!

They scutter like little gnomes to listen beneath the Staircase.

HARRY: Nine p.m. Dead on.

CHARLIE: Ssssh! Here she is!

(We hear clumping footsteps down the stairs. HARRY and CHARLIE follow the noise down with their eyes.)

Here's the typing bit.

(A MAN shouts in a loud voice off.)

MAN: *(Off.)* Thank you, Miss Ricard. I'll collect the manuscript tomorrow.

HARRY: Doorbang!

(The door bangs.)

CHARLIE: One, two, three, four, five...

HARRY: Sssh!

(The front door creaks. The footsteps creak up the stairs. Again CHARLIE and HARRY follow the noise with their eyes. They end up, craning their necks at the ceiling. There is a faint thud above.)

CHARLIE: There's her left boot!

HARRY: *(Returning to his chair and sitting.)* Oogh, I'll increase Miss Ricard's rent: that's a single bed-sitter.

CHARLIE: *(Moving C.)* Double-thumper now, Harry. Where were we?

HARRY: Doing my bla – pimple.

CHARLIE: *(Fetching some cotton wool from the shelves up C.)* Oh yes. *(He prods and presses at HARRY's face with lumps of cotton wool.)*

HARRY: Filthy habit. Filthy. Reckon Nature's all to cock, I do.

CHARLIE: Nature! Nature! Can't blame Nature for Miss Ricard. What! Local camp bicycle, she is. Blame the Industrial Revolution.

HARRY: I meant everyone. Whole arrangement. Mortifies me, Charlie – biology does.

CHARLIE: Oh Doctor Harry Leeds, M.D.

HARRY: Don't mention doctors! People treating them like Jesus; humping around in stethoscopes, discussing functions in loud pompous voices.

CHARLIE: And who told that filthy joke about a lesbian in the powder room?

HARRY: Oh, not jokes, Charlie! Don't mind a gag, I don't; but I believe...

CHARLIE: Where's the surgical spirit?

HARRY: Um, I was topping up the shaving lotion – um, in my cupboard...

(CHARLIE moves above HARRY's chair to the cupboard R, takes out a bottle of surgical spirit, returns to L of HARRY and dabs his face.)

It's just that I feel that Sex – all Sex could have been better arranged.

CHARLIE: You won't please rabbits with this, mate.

HARRY: Rabbits don't need to think. Don't suppose they even talk about it: *they* have nothing to talk *about,* don't you see?

CHARLIE: You what? You what! I should rub a dub!

HARRY: Oh, don't start arguing.

CHARLIE: Arguing! I reckon rabbits have nothing *else* to think about.

HARRY: Yes, but – what I mean – well, I think humans could have been made all the same.

CHARLIE: All men? No women, d'you mean?

HARRY: No, not completely. There'd have been sections of the community for feeding um, progeny and . . .

CHARLIE: Well! Get you for a communistic buttercup!

179

HARRY: I believe half Man's trouble's, due to Nature's reproductive systems, I do. I firmly believe this, Charlie. Oh,
you can scoff. But it should be nicer, cleaner, *prettier*. It
shouldn't be so folded up and sort of underneath.

CHARLIE: Juggling us about a bit, aren't you, dear! And
where, pray, should we keep our paraphernalia? On our
heads?

HARRY: And why not, *pray!* What's wrong with having, say,
a couple of antennas. Males. Females. The lot. Nothing
different or sniggery. Pleasant smile; raise your hat;
shake antennas; good laugh in the bargain.

CHARLIE: Oh lovely, dear! Lovely! Just what I fancy in the
morning – good laugh and shake me antennas. *(He
returns the bottle to its cupboard, and moves* C.)

*(HARRY rises, folds up his sheet, puts it on top of his cupboard,
then throws his towel into the basin R.)*

HARRY: There'd be no shame, I think. I think there'd be a
kind of – picturesqueness about antennas on folk's heads.
(His lip quivers slightly.) I shouldn't be as I am if it had
been an easy business – nice and clean and open.

CHARLIE: Starting our weeping stint, are we? Our weeping
stint?

HARRY: *(Strongly.)* No, we're not.

CHARLIE: Splendid! *(He sits in his chair LC.)*

*(HARRY brings the manicurist's table to R of CHARLIE, then the
stool, sits beside him and begins manicuring CHARLIE's nails.)*

Antennas, she wants! Antennas.

HARRY: Oh, shut your mouth. Keep the draught out.

CHARLIE: You're including greyhounds and alligators in this
system, I take it?

HARRY: All God's creatures.

CHARLIE: Poor old porcupine wouldn't know where to start.

HARRY: You don't care for anyone's feelings, you don't.

CHARLIE: I can just see crush hour – crush hour on the tube; pass down the car, raise your hat! Half the typing pool'd be on you for paternity.

HARRY: Oh no. Not at all. There'd be a method of folding them away during...

CHARLIE: Ha! Folding 'em up already! *(He jumps out of the chair, gleefully.)*

HARRY: Ah no...

CHARLIE: Folding 'em, dear! Folding 'em, you said.

HARRY: You ridicule everyone's high principles, *you* do!

CHARLIE: So I should think, when they stick antennas on crocodiles! *(He sits back in the chair.)*

(HARRY continues the manicuring.)

(After a while.) Started the old sulking stint, have we? Sulking stint?

HARRY: No.

CHARLIE: Because you ought to glory in God, you ought. What! Don't know what trouble is.

(HARRY sings the Hallelujah Chorus *under his breath.)*

– Should be sitting where I am, mate; dreading what the post may bring. Try *that* on your bloody hallelujahs!

HARRY: You're safe enough. No post on Sundays.

CHARLIE: They could *deliver* it, couldn't they?

HARRY: Thought you'd decided it was too late.

CHARLIE: That was Ronnie Unsworth; not me. They're forced to send a Summons within forty-eight hours, Ronnie Unsworth said.

HARRY: Must be twelve days, now.

CHARLIE: Thirteen. Mind me quick! *(He snatches his hand away.)*

(HARRY rises and moves L to the window.)

HARRY: I don't know what it's all for; just don't understand. If I was asked if I'd like to die – peacefully and – and beautifully – right now, I reckon I'd acquiesce. D'you fancy an hour's television?

CHARLIE: Blood, bowels and bestiality. No thanks.

HARRY: *(Pressing his nose to the green curtains.)* It's sort of wood-smokey outside; a night when your heels make chumf-chumfing noises as they bite the pavement. I can sense mist in the valleys; sheep coughing. Oh, church bells're so damn lonely.

CHARLIE: Sheep? Bells? We're backing on the gas works, mate.

HARRY: I was remembering young days; me and me sisters – used to run giggling to wash our faces in May dew.

CHARLIE: Coughing sheep and May dew! That was a quick winter.

(HARRY moves to the stockroom door and closes it, then replaces the stool and manicurist's table R.)

Oh hell! *(He rubs his face.)* If they'd only give me a sign. A sign. If they'd tell me it was cancelled, eh? Be such ecstasy, that would.

HARRY: Here! D'you fancy a bit of gardening?

CHARLIE: Middle of the night! On the mad stint, are we? Where, pray?

HARRY: In the yard.

CHARLIE: *Our* yard! They've written hymns about those satanic cobbles.

HARRY: There's Mum's seed boxes; switch on the stockroom light and it'd shine...

CHARLIE: No, no, no! Bluddyell – gardening! Grubby nails; earth worms snapping at your Wellingtons.

HARRY: Shall we go upstairs, then?

CHARLIE: *We? We?*

HARRY: What're *you* going to do, then?

CHARLIE: Stay in the shop. Lovely. I like it.

HARRY: There's nothing to do, Charlie.

CHARLIE: You what! There's mirrors to look in; swinging chairs; and all those pretty prophylactics to blow up. Lovely! *(He swings himself round in the chair.)*

HARRY: We've got some marzipan roll from yesterday's elevenses; and I could do a little brew-up.

CHARLIE: Mm. All right. If you like.

(He takes a letter from his pocket and reads.)

(HARRY moves down L and bustles with an electric kettle, filling it and plugging it in.)

HARRY: You know, last night I dreamt I was climbing a staircase. And I was naked except for a comb in me hair and a jock-strap.

CHARLIE: Well! Get "Bubbles".

HARRY: Thinking about holidays caused it. You know, we were saying how nice it'd be – tripping along some beach in a tiddly pair of briefs; people admiring our suntan. But we'd forgotten, Charlie; and last night I caught sight of myself in the bathroom mirror.

CHARLIE: *(Perusing his letter.)* D'you think she'll expect me to collect her at the station tomorrow? Cassy?

HARRY: *(Taking some marzipan roll from the shelf and unwrapping it.)* Anyhow, that'd be what caused the comb and jock-strap. 'Course, I knew it wasn't real – even in the dream. S'years since I woke up, clutching the quilt for shillin's. But I stepped out in this dream – stepped out and watched myself climb that staircase. It was horrible, Charlie. I saw a fat old man, bloated and hanging. I was flabby and ridiculous and I knew it. Paunch like a pig; freckled and grisly and...

CHARLIE: I'll be ill in a minute.

HARRY: Oh, you sardonic bitch! Easy for you: you've kept your looks. But I'm finished – even though I'm the same inside. I'm wearing tiddly briefs inside, Charlie, and my heart can still dance; but who knows it? Who'd want me on a beach? A yellowing sow's ear...

CHARLIE: Urgh, you're a messy talker ! Walk tall! Walk tall!

(HARRY puts tea in the pot.)

HARRY: I've given up expecting beneficence from you.

CHARLIE: Who're you kicking, eh? Who're you kicking? We're all depreciating, mate. What about my varicose veins? Varicose veins! Me legs're like fouled parrots' perches. Can hardly get my wind; and haven't seen me knee-caps since fifty-three. *(He swings out of his chair and moves R.)*

HARRY: But you're still beautiful on the surface, Charlie.

CHARLIE: *(Considering himself in the mirror R.)* Oh – I don't know.

HARRY: You are, Charlie. That's where you're lucky.

CHARLIE: I've kept myself in trim. Jowls wobble a bit.

HARRY: Doesn't show. *(He pours hot water into the pot.)*

CHARLIE: What d'you reckon Cassy'll think?

HARRY: She should be very proud.

CHARLIE: I didn't mean it that way. I meant – I meant us.

HARRY: *(Looking up.)* None of her business, is it?

CHARLIE: *(Nods.)* Thought we might close early tomorrow.

HARRY: Oh?

CHARLIE: If you wouldn't mind, Harry. I mean – 's'only every twenty years, eh? Father seeing his daughter for the first time.

HARRY: Quarter of a century.

CHARLIE: Don't exaggerate. She's only twenty-one or two. Ooogh, the conniving sow. Robbed me of my youth, she did.

HARRY: Cassy?

CHARLIE: No, her mother: only married me for the sheer purpose of – of begetting, as they'd have it in the Bible.

HARRY: And I will put enmity between thy seed and her seed.

CHARLIE: *(Moving LC.)* Eh? What's this, then?

HARRY: Somewhere in Genesis or Leviticus.

CHARLIE: On our religious stint, are we? Religious stint?

HARRY: Go on: I'm not stopping you talking.

CHARLIE: Forgotten where I was now.

HARRY: Grumbling, because you'd been a father: a privilege denied thousands of us.

CHARLIE: Privilege, was it! Oh, I should rub a dub, dear. What! Nine months of sick mornings, two bitchy weeks in Maternity – she flung me daffodils in a bedpan; and after an eternity of yowling, on me only silent night – there was a note pinned to the cot. Left me! They left me!

(HARRY pours the tea.)

Even me honeymoon was a – a – a holocaust: one night of passion and food-poisoning for thirteen. Maggots in the haddock, she claimed.

(HARRY giggles.)

Oh, I was laughing. Yes! What! Lovely – your blushing bride all shivering and turgid in the promenade shelter;

hurricanes whipping the shingle. Couldn't even paddle for a plague of jellyfish.

(HARRY roars with laughter. He gives CHARLIE his tea and leads him to his chair.)

HARRY: Come and have your tea, dear.

CHARLIE: *(Sitting in his chair.)* She had years of allotments, you know. Fifty bob a week, Harry, fifty bob, it was.

HARRY: Must've been a nasty divorce judge.

CHARLIE: Nasty – he wore a black cap, dear! Divorce hearing black cap! *(In a nasal voice.)* "Oh, we're in the Theatre, are we," he said. 'Course I was big time in those days, Harry. Played all the Number Ones. Don't think you realize just how big I was.

HARRY: Yes I do. *(He fetches his own tea and sits in his chair RC.)*

CHARLIE: Ask Archy Selder. Archy Selder'll tell you.

HARRY: Yes I know.

CHARLIE: Too true! But Theatre's a dirty word, see, Harry. Dirty word, it is. "Oh, we're in the Theatre, are we," he said, speaking on the verge of a burp. Well, I was young, see. Young, I was. And for a gag – a gag, that's all, Harry – I said: "We?" I said. "What pantomime are you in, then?"

HARRY: You never told me this.

CHARLIE: I didn't? Oh yes, dear. Brought the house down. Oogh, but the Judge went puce. Puce, he went. Bats fluttered from his ears. I reckon he doubled me allotment. *And* she got custody of the child. I was *robbed* of my child. Robbed! The most expensive joke *I* ever cracked.

HARRY: Oh – I can't see it. No. *(He shakes his head with indrawn breath.)*

CHARLIE: What's the doubt, then?

HARRY: Doesn't sound like English fairness to me.

CHARLIE: Fairness! You're not crouching there believing in
    Justice, you ramshackle twit! There's no Justice, mate;
    and never will be till we have computers on the Bench;
    and then I'll get one that needs oiling.

(HARRY still shakes his head.)

Look, stop shaking your head! *(Seeming strangely irritable.)*
What're you accusing me of, eh? Go on, say it!

HARRY: Say what?

CHARLIE: Oh belt up! *(He swings out of his chair and moves to the
    mirror L. He picks up the letter again and moves up C perusing
    it.)* *I* can't get Cassy into television, for heaven's sake.

HARRY: Must know someone she could meet.

CHARLIE: Who – the canteen manager? I've done one
    mingy commercial in ten years. Duffle coats. Sixteen
    guineas and four repeats. All I said was "Heave up the
    spinnaker!"

HARRY: Came over well.

CHARLIE: Yes; too well! This is the sow's *first* letter – except
    for that filthy postcard when I was late with her
    allotment; you know, when Mother had those vomiting
    spells. And just because I'm Networked wearing
    gumboots, yacht cap and royal blue bumfreezer,
    I'm wanted. Me daughter seeking fame. *And* Ronnie
    Unsworth's been sniffing around again.

HARRY: *(Rising and moving down L.)* Marzipan roll? *(He hands
    the plate of cake to CHARLIE.)*

CHARLIE: Ta. *(He takes a piece and moves above his chair.)*

*(HARRY replaces the cake, takes a piece himself, and returns to
his own chair.)*

Oh, it would come now, wouldn't it just! Police hanging
over my head and – d'you know I even had a begging
card addressed to the Duffle Coat Man? "Are you aware

of the many sick and needy mariners?" Haven't we any Eccles cake?

HARRY: You had it yesterday.

CHARLIE: Damn liar!

HARRY: I am not.

CHARLIE: Oh yes you are. Liar, mate!

HARRY: No, Charlie. *You* ate it whilst you were blow-waving that guitarist.

CHARLIE: Oh. *(He moves L and sits on the downstage end of the customers' bench.)* So, er – will you be going out at all, then?

HARRY: Why?

CHARLIE: When Cassy comes.

HARRY: Why should I?

CHARLIE: *(Shrugging.)* Well, she's my daughter.

HARRY: So?

CHARLIE: Nothing – nothing. *(He puts his marzipan roll on the bench beside him and picks up a magazine.)* Er – I can borrow Ronnie Unsworth's car any time I like.

HARRY: Oh yes? Borrow his car?

CHARLES: Might be an idea if we took your mother for a spin.

HARRY: *We?*

CHARLIE: Mm. She's stuck in the attic up there, isn't she, poor thing. Do her good – bit of a blow.

HARRY: She's seized with arthritis, Charles; can't move. *(He cocks a suspicious eye at* CHARLIE.*)*

CHARLIE: We could hoist her down the stairs; make a sort of um – cradle.

HARRY: Energetic all of a sudden, aren't we? Why this interest in Mum? You haven't mentioned her name in ten years.

CHARLIE: I beg yours. I beg yours! Bought her that pot plant for Christmas.

HARRY: Who carried it upstairs?

CHARLIE: Paralyzed, are you?

HARRY: Couldn't go near Mother, you said. Her slippers ponged, you said.

CHARLIE: That's – um – why I thought we should give her a bit of a blow.

HARRY: You think I'm simple! "Give Mother a blow!"

CHARLIE: It's no more than I'd do for my own mother – except she's stuck in that place; and I *visit* her, you see.

HARRY: When?

CHARLIE: Every Saturday.

HARRY: I meant when does my mother get her blow?

CHARLIE: Um...

HARRY: Tomorrow evening?

CHARLIE: Good idea! Lovely!

HARRY: Cassy's coming.

CHARLIE: She is? Oh, good gracious!

HARRY: Yes.

CHARLIE: Harry! Take her yourself. Ronnie Unsworth wouldn't mind.

HARRY: *(Rising and facing CHARLIE.)* Oogh, you send me right up the flue! Deceitful bitch! Hoist my mother down the landing! You'd as soon set fire to her drawers.

CHARLIE: Well, thank you, Vicar!

HARRY: I'm not one of your disc jockeys.

CHARLIE: Disc jockeys! Disc jockeys!

189

HARRY: Ashamed to have Harry meet your daughter? Well I'm telling you something: this is *my* shop; it's *my* life. If you're afraid of – of – of Cassy's accusing finger... *(He paces C.)* By God! You've more gall... ! If the Twelve Disciples were reincarnated, you'd arrange them in a pop group.

CHARLIE: *(Hurt.)* You're very frail tonight, mate.

HARRY: My mother's never said a harsh word about you. With all her pain and infirmity. "How's Charlie", she says.

CHARLIE: Why're you shoving your mother down my throat?

HARRY: She wouldn't "How's Charlie" if she knew you wanted to wrap her arthritis in a bloody block and tackle! *(He moves R to his basin, snatching up scissors and combs, throwing them down again, then round his chair to the shelves up C.)* D'you know, I hope the police clutch on you, dear! Teach you a lesson. Twisted bitch! By God, ashamed of his daughter meeting *me.*

CHARLIE: *(In almost a whisper.)* Nothing personal.

(HARRY moves down L and plugs in the kettle again.)

HARRY: Oogh, you're all intertwined, Charlie. *(Moving C.)* One great big tube of non-sequitur.

(HARRY's turn of spirit gives us a first suspicion that CHARLIE is not always top dog. CHARLIE is subdued for a while. He "walks" his fingers along the bench.)

CHARLIE: I'd meet her at the station, Harry, but um – we haven't a clue what each other looks like.

HARRY: Wear your duffle coat, dear! Carry a copy of *Boys' Own* under your arm.

CHARLIE: Ha, yes. No – um, I'd rather – you know – meet her in private, really. By myself here.

HARRY: Should've thought of that before, as Nanny used to say.

CHARLIE: Thought've what?

HARRY: *(Shrugging.)* *You* got married; *you* had the daughter. Well, now you've got *me*!

CHARLIE: *(Rising.)* Yeah; don't I know it. *(He moves disconsolately to the window.)*

HARRY: Yes – me! Dirty Harry Leeds, who fed you; taught you a trade when you flopped in the theatre.

CHARLIE: I beg yours! I beg yours! Couple more commercials, I'd be on top again.

HARRY: Pull the other, dear!

CHARLIE: Archy SeIder only has a Series lined up for me, that's all! Just my own Series, dear!

HARRY: Really! You'll be turning in your clippers, then.

CHARLIE: What! I should rub a dub!

HARRY: Moving into the Hilton.

CHARLIE: Penthouse, mate. Penthouse!

HARRY: *(Moving to the front door up c.)* Good! I'll clear out your side of the wardrobe.

CHARLIE: *(Moving up c to HARRY.)* You what! Can't wait till the body's cold? Can't wait till the body's cold?

HARRY: Well, we mustn't hold you back, Charlie! I'll chuck your stuff down.

CHARLIE: It's the middle of Sunday night, you twit.

HARRY: That's right.

CHARLIE: Where would I go?

HARRY: Straight into the Hilton, Charlie. You can interview Cassy in your Hartnell Suite.

CHARLIE: Oh the hell with Cassy! What're we bitching about?

HARRY: Because I'm too sordid for you.

CHARLIE: Oh shut the door, and calm down. Kettle's boiling.

(He picks up his cup from the bench.)

(HARRY closes the door and moves down L. He pours water into the teapot.)

HARRY: I'd've given my back teeth to be married.

CHARLIE: *(Holding out his cup.)* Who'd want your dirty old back teeth!

HARRY: *(Filling CHARLIE's cup with milk and tea.)* It's caused me more embarrassment: the filthy questions they asked...

CHARLIE: Who asked?

HARRY: "Are you clean, Mr Leeds?" – "D'you live with your mother?" – "Who was that young man I saw you with last night?"

CHARLIE: Who's this? Who's this? Eh? Eh?

HARRY: *(Pouring his own tea.)* The mothers – parents – when I had that Scout Troop.

CHARLIE: Oh.

HARRY: And my face flamed up; always blushed. I could see it coming: they'd stop me in the street. A bit of yack-yack, then slam below the belt: "Are you married?" And they had that raised eyebrow'd purposeful disinterest. "No, I fear not" – "Oh-oh-oh-oh, aren't you! Mm, well little Johnny tells us *everything that happens*, Mr Leeds. And my face like the backside of a gibbon.

CHARLIE: Oh well. Never mind. *(He picks up his marzipan roll and sits in his chair.)*

HARRY: How dare they! How damn dare they!

CHARLIE: You're not tying yourself in knots, for God's sake? It's twenty years ago.

HARRY: *(Going to sit in his chair.)* It leaves a scar.

CHARLIE: Yes; well I shouldn't've trusted you, either. There never was such a short-trousered nobble-knee'd piker. Shouldn't've trusted you with me stuffed otter.

HARRY: You never saw me in my scouting days.

CHARLIE: Never saw you! Never saw you! That first trip – very first trip – Hampton Court – your mother made us brawn butties.

HARRY: I had my new suède jacket...

CHARLIE: You had your full khaki, dear. The lot. Long socks, dagger *and* a pole, no less. Talk about embarrassed!

(HARRY giggles shyly.)

HARRY: Mm, I've always had a guilty conscience. Can't think why I went in uniform.

CHARLIE: Oh, you admit it *now*.

HARRY: We-ell. I didn't know you then. Suppose I felt important; manly. Putting on a bit of style, I suppose.

CHARLIE: And as for the Maids of Honour Shop ! You! Ordering a cream tea in French.

HARRY: *(Giggling.)* Yes. That was another time I blushed –

CHARLIE: – ducked under the table –

HARRY: – pretended I'd dropped a spoon.

CHARLIE: Yes: you were gone ten minutes. Thought you'd had a come-over.

HARRY: My blushes lasted longer than Worcester sauce in a church cupboard.

CHARLIE: Oh, get Rudyard Kipling! What! Witty, dear.

HARRY: Long time since I last blushed, Charlie.

CHARLIE: I don't know why – with that lot wound on your head. *(He nods at HARRY's bandages.)*

HARRY: Oh, don't start on that, Charlie. Please!

CHARLIE: You're a silly old twit, aren't you! *(Fondly.)* By hell you are. *(He munches his marzipan roll.)*

(HARRY sips his tea: then, right out of the blue –)

HARRY: I once went in a brothel.

CHARLIE: Right in the middle of me Battenburg!

HARRY: It shows I've been around.

CHARLIE: Go in khaki shorts, did you?

HARRY: No.

CHARLIE: Dagger and pole? Get a new badge for that, don't you?

HARRY: Give over, will you!

CHARLIE: Don't say you weren't issued with your Brothel Badge, mate! It's worn on the left arm between the one for getting knotted and the one for rubbing sticks together. Lovely! Sort of field of azure with a pair of discarded knickers on a tent pole.

HARRY: *(Angrily.)* Oh belt up with your sneering, you sardonic runt!

CHARLIE: Thank you, Hilaire Belloc! We do turn nasty! Nice kick-up-the-hooter for someone who's merely trying to keep life cheery.

HARRY: Oogh, you're so deep! D'you think I don't realize how vicious you are underneath? All your cod jocularity with its slimy undertow. Needling, digging, cutting. Oh go to hell! *(After a pause.)* I was telling you something interesting...

CHARLIE: I've heard it. Ten times I've heard your brothel tale.

HARRY: Damn liar.

CHARLIE: There was a man weeping on the staircase. Right?

HARRY: That's only part of it.

CHARLIE: Then a door flung open.

HARRY: Curtain. It was a curtain.

CHARLIE: And a woman with a cigarette burning her lips asked you to dance naked while she threw marmalade at your navel. I've heard it, mate. Heard it. You've nothing left I haven't seen and heard a thousand times – and you always end it the same way.

HARRY: End what?

CHARLIE: Your brothel tale. You pause; suck in your breath; and say, "How's that for Holy Week?" *(He flings his marzipan roll in his basin.)* And if I once more hear you pause, suck in your breath, and say "How's that for Holy Week?", I'll stuff a skewer in me ear and go to hell as a kebab!

(There is a pause.)

HARRY: I never know where I am with you, Charlie. One minute to the next; never know where I am.

CHARLIE: Spice of life.

HARRY: Have you ever thought about my name, Charlie: Harry Leeds? Harry C. Leeds. How d'you spell it?

CHARLIE: Going off your rocker?

HARRY: How d'you know I'm here? What proof have you that I exist? How d'you know I'm not imaginary?

(The door bell rings. CHARLIE and HARRY rise. They stand in silence. After a while it rings again.)

HARRY: They wouldn't come on a Sunday. It's Sunday.

CHARLIE: *(His voice trembling.) Might* be Ronnie Unsworth.

HARRY: You'll have to go.

(The door bell rings.)

They'll only keep on and on.

CHARLIE: You go. Peep through the keyhole.

(Both of them move to the door up C. CHARLIE opens it, and HARRY moves into the lobby. After a while he returns.)

Man, is it?

HARRY: Yes.

CHARLIE: Policeman?

HARRY: Can't tell. He's standing in front of the keyhole.

CHARLIE: Oh, come out! *(He pulls HARRY aside, to R of the door, then goes out into the lobby. After a second he returns, holding both hands over his mouth.)*

HARRY: Is it?

CHARLIE: *(Nodding.)* Policeman. Saw him through the keyhole.

HARRY: What's he doing?

CHARLIE: Nodding and smiling.

HARRY: Who at?

CHARLIE: *Me*, you fool! *(He closes the door.)* He's crouched on the other side.

HARRY: What now?

CHARLIE: Bluff it out. Switch out the lights.

HARRY: Wait! He's opening the door!

(A tall shadow can be seen through the glass of the door. Soon there is a knock.)

CHARLIE: God help us all and Oscar Wilde.

VOICE: *(Off.)* Anyone there!

CHARLIE: *(Calling.)* We're closed! Come tomorrow! *(He pushes HARRY downstage.)*

(CHARLIE and HARRY whisper together.)

VOICE: *(Off.)* Will you open up, please.

(CHARLIE creeps back. Tentatively he opens the door a few inches.)

Mr Charles Dyer at home, sir?

CHARLIE: Possibly. Possibly. Why?

VOICE: *(Off.)* Would *you* be Mr Charles Dyer?

CHARLIE: I'm a ratepayer, Officer. I mean, how do I know um, um. I've a right to see your identity card.

VOICE: *(Off.)* Certainly, sir. Although it's quite unnecessary.

(A uniformed arm is seen – holding a card. CHARLIE looks at it; the hand is withdrawn, and CHARLIE closes the door.)

CHARLIE: *(Whispering.)* He's got a card.

HARRY: What's it say?

CHARLIE: *(Hopelessly.)* Didn't like to look.

HARRY: Oh, you're rotten weak, you are.

(There is another knock on the glass. CHARLIE slowly opens the door.)

VOICE: *(Off.)* *Are* you Mr Dyer, sir?

(CHARLIE nods glumly.)

CHARLIE: *(Whispering.)* Yes.

VOICE: *(Off.)* Ah. There we are then, sir. Good night.

(The POLICEMAN hands CHARLIE a long buff envelope, then clumps away. The outside door bangs.)

(CHARLIE closes the shop door and wanders down L.)

HARRY: *(Following him.)* I'd never've believed they'd deliver it on Sunday. *(He pats CHARLIE's shoulders.)* *It'll* all work out.

CHARLIE: *(In a tiny voice.)* Yes.

HARRY: Um, what's it say?

(CHARLIE, his fingers trembling, opens the envelope. He takes out an official paper and tries to read it; then he gives it to HARRY.)

CHARLIE: You read it, Harry.

HARRY: Oh um, are you sure you want me to?

CHARLIE: It's a blur, Harry – all a blur, like seeing it in triplicate.

Here...! *(He hands over the document.)*
(HARRY begins reading it aloud, moving C and fumbling for his spectacles.)

HARRY: Um – "Inforrnation has been laid this day by Rychard Lees, Chief Constable..."

CHARLIE: *(Moving below his chair.)* Yes, yes. Skip to the meat.

HARRY: *(Reading.)* Um... Oh God! Listen, Charlie. "...that you did at the County Borough aforesaid at an establishment known as The Adam's Apple behave in a manner likely to cause a serious breach of the peace and did parade in female attire..." Oh God, Charlie!

CHARLIE: Read it, Harry! Read it!

HARRY: *(Reading.)* "... and did importune in a manner calculated to bring – depravity..."
(CHARLIE sinks into his chair. HARRY is himself near to tears.)
Oh hell, Charlie. *(Whispering.)* Oh hell.

CHARLIE: Woosh – they've – they've really come thundering into Jordan, haven't they! I should rub-a-woosh! *(He looks old, tired, frightened.)*

HARRY: Oh Charlie!

CHARLIE: When does it say?

HARRY: *(Reading.)* "You are therefore summoned to appear before the Magistrates' Court sitting at the..."

CHARLIE: The date, dear! Date! I don't care if they're sitting on their potties. Get to the date!

HARRY: *(Reading.)* Yes. Um – blah blah blah – twenty-third of this month.

(CHARLIE and HARRY both count silently.)

CHARLIE: Ten days' time.

HARRY: Nine. No, ten. Yes.

CHARLIE: 'F'only I could go now – tonight; get it done.
Fourteen days torture already, Harry; and now another
ten. Harry, read it again...

*(In a sudden vicious movement, HARRY tears the summons and
flings it down.)*

HARRY: *(Moving RC.)* Goddam you, Charlie!

(CHARLIE rises and kneels to retrieve the torn pieces.)

CHARLIE: What're you – what're you... !

HARRY: Never told me all this, did you! "A mistake", it was
– "victimization" – everyone shopping poor innocent
Charlie.

CHARLIE: You trying to scuttle me? *(He moans over the torn
papers.)* There'll be a law against this.

HARRY: Putting on drag – you forgot that bit!

CHARLIE: Drag! Drag?

HARRY: Parading in female att...

CHARLIE: It was me cabaret act, dear. Me old panto act. I
borrowed the cigarette-girl's jumper; gave her a quid;
pinched a hat and rolled up me trousers. *(He rises.)*
There's your drag, mate, I swear it. Oh, and I wrapped
a tartan rug round for a skirt. Call that "drag"? Tell me!
Honest!

HARRY: *(Moving C.)* And *after* you sat on Ed Chryslar's knee?

CHARLIE: You what! Oh, I should rub a dub: he's only
married with five kids, dear!

(HARRY snatches the paper from CHARLIE's hand.)

HARRY: *(Wearily.)* I'll mend it. *(During the following dialogue, he
searches the drawers and shelves up C, looking for sticky tape.)*

CHARLIE: *(Sitting in his chair.)* There's nothing wrong with Ed Chryslar, Harry. Nothing. Five kids. Five! He may have another by now.

HARRY: *Yours*, Charlie?

CHARLIE: *(Between his teeth.)* Cut that out! I'm telling you – Ed Chryslar married that sexy bit on the whatcher-me-call-it Show. Lovely girl. And he bet me five pounds I wouldn't do me impersonation of Lady Muck launching a battleship. *(Falsetto.)* And All Who Sail In Her – you know that old thing I do. A gag, Harry. A straightup gag, dear; and this stupid young copper – only a boy, Harry.

Only a boy, he was... *(Pointing to the shelves down L.)* There's the sticky tape.

HARRY: *(Moving L.)* Oh yes. *(He cuts the tape and pieces the document together.)*

CHARLIE: It was so quick, you see. So quick. Policemen by the cartload: up the plugholes, under the skirting. Someone complained, you see. Rowdyism. That delicatessen next door. Ugly yob! Strike me dead if I even *sniff* another gherkin! There was nothing happening, you see; that was the trouble. We-e-ll, they daren't send coppers for nothing; wasting official petrol; so they stamped on Charlie! Oh yes. What! Run him in, dear – he's better than nothing. *(He shivers and rubs his arms.)* Someone walked over me grave. *(He tries to laugh.)* In fact, they're marking time.

(HARRY gives him the mended summons.)

Oh, that's lovely, Harry. Nicely done. Ta. Ta.

(HARRY nods, replaces the tape, and sits downstage on the bench.)

Whew! *(He rises, trying to subdue another fit of shivering.)* You believe me, don't you, Harry? Y-y-you do believe me?

HARRY: *(Nodding.)* Yes, but – but why did they take your name?

CHARLIE: *(Moving C, then standing above his chair.)* It was this young copper, Harry. You see – I was on Ed Chryslar's knee and I pushed me t-t-tongue out and said, "Yarboo, arrest me!" – or something. You know what? *He bloody did!* This young copper. Kept pushing me; p-pushing me, Harry. People watching. Wretched, Harry – it w-was wretched. "Aw, come off!" I said. I said: "I'm old enough to be your father; your daddy," I said. "*Please*, I said. "Please, son... !" *(He drops his voice to a whisper. There are tears in his eyes.)* They were going to put me in the Black M-Maria, Harry. If it hadn't been for the Inspector – nice elderly man – he checked me driving licence; sent me home. *(He wipes his eyes; blows his nose; then he forces himself into the attack.)* But, by God, I'll prove 'em wrong! What! "May it please your Honour! I am an established member of the theatrical profession. Yes! *Profession, sir! And* a married man. Yes sir ! *Married*!"

HARRY: Long time ago.

CHARLIE: I was married, mate. That's me. Nothing puffy with me, mate. *I'm normal. I* was married *with a baby.*

HARRY: Whom you haven't seen in twenty years. She's coming tomorrow, isn't she!

CHARLIE: Angel of doom! Are you *trying* to hang me? Trying to hang me, are you? Why don't you help me; give me some confidence? Because I *am* innocent, Harry. I *was* doing my old panto stuff. "Ladies and Gentlemen of the Jury..." Hear me through on this, Harry; pick holes; say what you like. I'll keep practising until the day. Oh, I'll prove 'em wrong. I'll prove 'em... "Ladies and Gentlemen of the Jury. Your Honour. I am an established member of the Theatrical Profession in good standing." – God, it's lucky I kept up me Equity! Right up to date – "Your Honour, my whole act is based upon the uproarious antics of my female impersonations. Top line. Top line female impersa – um – Was Dan Leno a puff? Was Henry Ainley? The great W. S. Pennington. Charlie's Aunt; all these wonderful names? No, sir. No, sir, old lad! Only five years since I made my farewell debut; they cheered. They stood and cried out: "Encore, Charlie!" – um, fifteen years, maybe... *(He stops; plucks his lip.)* Harry, when did I do that Broker's Man at Streatham?

HARRY: Before the War?

CHARLIE: Oh God! Oh hell! *(He covers his mouth with his hand. He speaks in a tiny, quiet voice.)* "Ladies and Gentlemen of the Jury, I'm a small-time back-street hairdresser; and I don't know why I – just a gag; bit of fun! Please give me a break."

(HARRY rises and moves LC.)

HARRY: You've done all those little film bits; and that commercial.

CHARLIE: *(Shrugging him off and moving away C.)* I know. I know. Which – um –which commercial?

HARRY: The duffle coat one. Everyone'd know that.

CHARLIE: Yes, but um – I needed one where I was – well, where I was dressed as a woman – to prove my case. But it's getting on for thirty years, Harry. I can hardly say I was rehearsing, can I? By hell, this'll ruin me Come-Back.

(HARRY sits in CHARLIE's chair LC.)

HARRY: Don't fret, Charlie. It'll be all right.

CHARLIE: *(Spiritedly.)* You needn't bolster me, dear. I'm not bothered. I'll handle my own case, that's why. What'm I in the theatre for? Eh? I'll tell 'em! I'll show I'm an old pro. God, if I can't use my personality to – to... *(He shakes his head.)* Oh Christ, Harry, I'm so f-frightened. *(He flops at HARRY's feet.)*

(HARRY cradles CHARLIE in his lap, stroking his head and rocking him backwards and forwards.)

HARRY: Don't fret, CHARLIE: Don't fret. We'll see. We'll – see, Charlie.

CHARLIE: I'm innocent, Harry. Innocent.

HARRY: Oh Charlie – you poor old bugger

CHARLIE: Yes. *(He sits back on his haunches. He tries to smile.)* D'you ever see two such frail old twits!

HARRY: But you won't be alone, Charlie; at the trial. I'll come with you.

CHARLIE: You! Come with me? God no, they'd give me ninety years.

CURTAIN

SCENE 2

The same. Half an hour later.

When the CURTAIN rises, CHARLIE is discovered slumped in his chair, a shawl round his shoulders, thoroughly woe-begone. Every now and then he gives a sob; his eyes are red. The front door bangs (Off.). Then HARRY enters. He wears a macintosh which is dripping, and a sou-wester over his bandages. For a while he stands up c, stamping his feet and blowing water from his face; brushing the rain from his raincoat. Then he moves down C and hands CHARLIE a packet of aspirins.

HARRY: Had to go all the way to that machine on the corner.

CHARLIE: You'd've got 'em at the pub, stupid twit.

HARRY: *(Hedging.)* Could I?

CHARLIE: Where's the gin? You haven't forgotten the gin?

HARRY: They were closed, you see. Pub was closed.

CHARLIE: Not the back door.

HARRY: I didn't like. I'm – I'm no good at back doors, Charlie. You go for some.

CHARLIE: Oh yes! God lighting fires under me sinuses – I feel like traipsing through floods for gin! I should rub a dub. *(He chews two aspirins, grimacing.)* Better make some of your lousy char to wash 'em down.

HARRY: Surely. *(He hangs his damp clothes in the stock room.)*

CHARLIE: There's a smell of gas in there. Reckon that jet's blown out again.

HARRY: No, it hasn't.

CHARLIE: Smells like it. Just the right size for a tomb, that stock room.

HARRY: *(Moving R of CHARLIE.)* Might be handy at a pinch.

CHARLIE: That kind of talk's against God, Harry. Oh yes, dear. Hallelujah or no hallelujah, let's keep the jet going. I should rub a dub.

HARRY: Your eyes aren't half red.

CHARLIE: Only the white parts.

(CHARLIE turns away, but HARRY leans forward to see.)

Keep to yourself! You look like a pregnant hen. Have you seen your hips? Have you? Ever seen 'em? Far too wide for a man. Oh yes. A real man has great broad withers which taper to powerful flanks: what one might call the crutch of the matter. And look at you! Hen is too delicate a term. Um, pelican! Yes! You're a pregnant pelican, mate. *(He has another look at HARRY: He points to HARRY's bandages.)* Bit much when you even pad sou'westers with 'em!

HARRY: I feel safer. Have you worked anything out?

CHARLIE: Have I hell! I'm right in it, dear. No escape: I've as much chance of shoving straw in the pouch of a thirst-maddened wallaby. Anyway, sufficient unto the day, mate. I should care.

(HARRY moves above CHARLIE and looks in the tea tin down L.)

I'm innocent. Oh, belt up reminding me!

HARRY: Oh – we've used all the tea; unless Mum has a spot in her cupboard.

CHARLIE: No! Don't! Let's leave – sleeping things up there.

(HARRY takes a bar of chocolate from the shelf.)

HARRY: Here! How about some drinking chocolate?

CHARLIE: Yes.

(HARRY scutters childishly in the corner down L, plugging in the kettle and unwrapping his bar of chocolate.)

(Out of the blue.) You needn't start increasing the rent, Harry.

HARRY: Whose rent? Mother doesn't charge you rent.

CHARLIE: *You*, mate! *You* needn't increase the rent.

HARRY: *(Tetchily.)* I'm not with you, Charlie. Spell it for me: 's'too early in the morning for obscurity.

CHARLIE: I mean don't slop and slap in the pity of it all; don't talk nice and *be* nice; and above all, dear – above all, don't expect anything for it – no tail wagging.

(HARRY starts shredding chocolate into a cup.)

Because – *(His voice trembles, but he pulls himself together.)* – because I'll be giving you nothing, mate. *(He rises and stretches largely.)* Aye-yi-yi yi-yi! Soon be dawn, I reckon. *(He moves to HARRY.)* What're you up to?

(HARRY does not answer.)

Eh? What's all this?

HARRY: If you had a teeniest scrap of thought for anyone; if you had...

CHARLIE: Very well, I'm sorry. I'm sorry. I'm sorry. But no preaching, please! What're you messing at?

HARRY: *(After a deep sigh.)* I'm shredding this chocolate bar, like – like me and my sisters used to do. Long after midnight – sneaking downstairs for hot water – all of us giggling. And my auntie, too; she was with us; she's alive still. She only has six skins. You're supposed to have seven; but auntie's only got six.

CHARLIE: She rides low in the saddle.

HARRY: Oh, you silly bitch! *(He giggles.)*

(CHARLIE smiles slightly.)

CHARLIE: God help us all and Oscar Wilde. I'm living with a schoolgirl. *(At HARRY.)* Are we going to suck-suck scrumchy choccy, are we?

(HARRY pours hot water into his concoction. CHARLIE watches and shudders.)

Urrgh, it looks vile! Like some ghastly brew for the Circumcision Rites of the dreaded Mumba Wumbas.

(HARRY licks his lips uneasily. CHARLIE pushes home his advantage.)

D'you like cooking, dear? Do you, love? Catch me drinking *that*! I tell you, Harry, you're a dizzy Lizzy. All soft. Your hands're soft; your shoulders are soft; and your hips are too wide for a man.

HARRY: And you repeat yourself. You say everything twice.

CHARLIE: Who does? Who does?

HARRY: There you are! A double "who does".

CHARLIE: We-ell.

HARRY: Think your every word is so divine, everyone – including God, is panting for a duplicate.

CHARLIE: *(Haughtily.)* Really, Well, for your information, tit-face, *you* just said "every" twice; and you've an exasperating twitch at mealtimes.

HARRY: Little mannerisms...

CHARLIE: Mannerisms! Mannerisms! I've had twenty years of that hole in your face and no sooner do you put a fork near it than you sniff and jerk your head to the left. *(He demonstrates.)* Like that! I'll do it again. Up comes the fork... *(He does it two or three times.)* Sniff; jerk; stuff! Sniff; jerk; stuff! An outright twitch, dear. What! Touch of the palsy, mate! That's you. Probably degenerate into a sniffing, jerking, stuffing jelly. *(Moving below his chair.)* Want to watch it, dear; bits and pieces'll begin dropping off because of the vibration. *(He sits and swings round in his chair, laughing.)*

HARRY: At least, I don't cut my toe-nails in the kitchen.

CHARLIE: Once! Once in all my life.

HARRY: It was enough.

CHARLIE: And who never empties the teapot?

HARRY: *(Moving L of* CHARLIE's *chair.)* And who leaves the basin filthy and never washes her razor?

CHARLIE: *(Yelling.)* She hasn't time! After you've hogged the closet for hours, puffing yourself up! So help me – if ever I reach heaven, there'll be two toilets!

HARRY: And if I reach heaven, someone else'll be cleaning them.

CHARLIE: Heaven! *You!* Ha! On second thoughts, yes: I can just visualize you – a bleached poppy in a coterie of deceased giggling gentlemen; illuminated wolf cubs saluting in a pink mist of cherubimic bottoms and sugar lumps. And by Hell, Harry, if I'm Up There – I'll jump slap in the middle of you all – *and belch*! *(He swings round and round in his chair, rubbing his hands in evil anticipation.)*

HARRY: *(Dryly.)* We shan't be taken aback – having heard rumours of your arrival.

(CHARLIE swings his chair to a stop and surveys HARRY.)

CHARLIE: Mmm. On our smug stint, are we? Our slightly-gloating stint?

HARRY: More your line, Charlie.

CHARLIE: You're an insidious creep, aren't you! Enigma – enigma's the word; sometimes a willowy thing giggling at big words and sometimes a clutching goblin with a goat on your navel. You've got me. I see it now.

HARRY: Oh. It's all my fault, is it?

CHARLIE: You're dead right, it is. Dead right! Twenty years you've had me. There I am – doing fine. Empress. Third on the Bill ! You pick me up in a Maids of Honour shop; and you *did* pick me up, Harry – with your dagger and scout pole.

HARRY: *(Pityingly.)* Oh no, Charlie. No.

CHARLIE: *You picked me up!* And matriculated me to the glory of a two-bit back-street barber.

HARRY: I came down to see if I could help. *(Moving towards the door.)* I'm not staying.

CHARLIE: You came down to gloat, mate! To rub your hands, to lick your lips; to taste the shame and excitement, without any of the danger. Oooogh, he's going to Court; he's going to Court; Charlie's going to Court! "I'll come with you, Charlie," he said! "You won't be alone!" *I'll be the loneliest old bugger on earth! (He pushes his fist to his mouth and pauses to control himself.)* You'll be there – my daughter'll be there – the old sow'll be there – and I'll be the lonelist ex-Third-on-the-Bill on the bill. What! I should rub a dub. *(He thumps the arm of his chair.)* And I'm *innocent*, I'm *innocent*!

HARRY: *(Moving down C towards him.)* Charlie...

CHARLIE: Get off! Get away! Get back to your stinking pit, dear. The show's over. Midnight matinee. Over. Finished.

(HARRY moves to the door.)

(Yelling after him.) And all God's children have toe-nails! All of 'em! It's a kind of thin horn, provided by the Almighty, for the protection of our digits. There is nothing rude or disgusting. Queen Victoria had 'em; you have 'em; and all the ladies in your Presbyterian Church Choir have 'em-except that bitch who sings the solos; and she has hooves.

(HARRY moves down to him.)

HARRY: All this is vengeance, pure and simple. You won't be told; you won't be helped; you're never wrong, and if you're in a hole you drag everyone down with you.

CHARLIE: This is *you* we're describing, mate!

HARRY: *You* started it with the teapot.

CHARLIE: I beg yours. I beg yours! You said I repeated myself.

HARRY: You said I twitched.

CHARLIE: Toe-nails! Toe-nails!

HARRY: And I say it again. As long as I'm cooking and scrubbing –

CHARLIE: Great! Here comes the hot-washing-machine stint!

HARRY: – as long as I'm cooking and scrubbing for you, Charlie, you can keep your filthy nail clippings out of my kitchen. Period! *(He moves to the door.)* I'll bet Victoria never cut her nails in the kitchen.

(HARRY exits up C, slamming the door. CHARLIE rises, hurries to the door, opens it, and yells upstairs.)

CHARLIE: No – she did 'em in the Music Gallery! *(He slams the door, then opens it again and shouts.)* Harry! *Harry*!!

(HARRY returns.)

HARRY: Sssh! What?

CHARLIE: *(Indicating the shop.)* It's – so quiet; so much room for thoughts. I um, don't mind risking my life with some of that – black brew. *(He sits in his chair.)*

HARRY: *(Moving down L.)* Don't do me any favours, dear.

(A silence follows. HARRY potters. He mixes hot water with his concoction – to freshen it, then he pours two mugsful, and brings one to CHARLIE.)

CHARLIE: No sugar?

(HARRY sighs. He returns to the table with the mugs, puts sugar in each, then comes back to CHARLIE. CHARLIE grabs his drink. HARRY goes and sits in his chair with his own mug. They both take some while before actually sipping, and afterwards, HARRY's face lights with pleasure. The drink is a success! But CHARLIE merely grunts; and after a few sips, he nods at HARRY's bandages.)

When're they coming off, then?

HARRY: I will take them off, Charlie. I – er...

CHARLIE: When? When?

HARRY: *(Shaking his head.)* A – a bit longer. Charlie. I feel safe with these, you see. Be awful without them now – empty – unclean.

(CHARLIE sighs deeply. He looks around the shop.)

CHARLIE: We had such wonderful plans, didn't we!

HARRY: Yes.

CHARLIE: Wonderful plans, we had.

HARRY: *(Nodding.)* Hydraulic chairs; shell-shaped basins –

CHARLIE: – wrought iron on the bloody striped pole –

HARRY: – tinted mirrors; and that boy with the hairy arms'd've painted us murals.

CHARLIE: Could have expanded upstairs: salon de dames. Tea and crumpet under the driers.

HARRY: Parfums; boutiques.

CHARLIE: Branches in Bond Street –

HARRY: – Muswell Hill –

CHARLIE: Muswell Hill!! Are you mad?

HARRY: 'S'part of the set-up. All the nobs have suburban branches. Make a packet, dear.

CHARLIE: Right. Muswell Hill.

HARRY: Paris. Brussels.

CHARLIE: Amsterdam. New York!

HARRY: And then me hair falls out! Bluddyell!

(HARRY sits groaning, but CHARLIE – lips licked wickedly, eyes gleaming with evil relish – begins to recount –.)

CHARLIE: I was telling your mother: "Overnight, Mrs Leeds", I said. "There it was," I said, "on his pillow." Oh, the shock! "Harry," I shouted. "Your hair, mate! Look at your suffering hair. On the pillow!" I should rub a dub. You went white. Did you know you went white and started screaming?

HARRY: *(Nodding.)* Like finding me own eyeball. That's the only way I could describe it to someone like you, Charlie, who still has hair. Think how you'd feel, finding your eye looking at you and one side of your face all black.

CHARLIE: Urrgh. You always were a messy talker. No breeding; no culture.

HARRY: I was trying to make you appreciate...

CHARLIE: I don't have to appreciate empty eye sockets, mate. It was me wakened you, wasn't it?

HARRY: *(Nodding.)* Horrible.

CHARLIE: Thought it was a kitten curled on your pillow. "Where did he get a kitten?" I thought. I was going to stroke it. Stroke it, dear! *(He puts out his hand and draws it back.)* Oh my God! Well, you always did have a funny head, Harry. I mean, you did, dear; but all hairless! Like a washerwoman's elbow, it was.

HARRY: Can't you shut up! Call yourself a friend – knowing how I suffer?

CHARLIE: *(Casting his glance at the ceiling and muttering.)* Now for the great martyr stint.

HARRY: Ever since my first little bare patch it's been the same. It was you who first told me. D'you remember? "Oogh, you're going bald," you said. "D'you know?" Of course I bloody knew. I wanted to forget, not be reminded. *(He rises, takes his mug to the basin R and washes it.)* People don't realize it's an affliction like anything else.

CHARLIE: Really? Cause you great pain, does it? Great pain – falling hair?

HARRY: *(Moving C.)* The pain's in here and up here! *(He taps his heart and head.)* A little understanding, that's all, Charlie. You don't rush up to a limping man and say: "Hey, you've only one leg, did you know?" You're all polite; you make excuses: "Really? I never knew you had tin legs, wall eyes and a goitre." But see a bald man and it's everybody's tee-hee time. "Your head's coming through your hair, mate!" "Hello, Curly!" "Hey, want your bonce polished for two-pence ?" Being bald's an affliction. A human problematic affliction.

CHARLIE: Too blasted true! It's afflicting you, afflicting me, the business, everything.

HARRY: Wish we'd made it a car accident now; or a bandit with a cosh. You talked me into a falling beam.

CHARLIE: All our customers appreciate this is old property. Nothing more natural than a bit of woodworm in the cellar. Not that you can live for ever swathed in swaddling.

HARRY: 'S' only seven weeks.

CHARLIE: *Only*! D'you know what Ronnie Unsworth said yesterday? "Is it my imagination," he said, "or are Harry's bandages getting bigger?"

HARRY: He didn't, did he?

CHARLIE: Harry, they *are* getting bigger! Each fresh morning sees another layer. Talk about woodworm – more like you've been trampled by bison. And you've a beautiful wig in there you refuse to wear. *(He nods at the stock room.)* A beautiful wig.

HARRY: It doesn't work, Charlie. *(Moving down L with the mug.)* I've tried it. *(He puts the mug on the shelf.)*

CHARLIE: You're worse than Fanny with her first bottom set!

HARRY: *(Moving above CHARLIE's chair to C.)* I've nothing to join it to, d'you see? My neck's naked, Charlie.

CHARLIE: *(Putting his mug on the floor.)* Bit of scribble round the edges with an eyebrow pencil. Perishing barber who can't sketch a tuft of hair. I'll do it for you myself. Now.

(CHARLIE rises and lunges at HARRY, who backs off R, squealing and cuddling his arms over his head. CHARLIE follows.)

No disgrace, y'know – alopecia. Bishops get alopecia. A well-known thing – alopecia. Alopecia is...

HARRY: *(Yelling.)* Will you shut up! Carping swine. *(Quietly.)* I might try tomorrow. I'll remove the bandages and...

CHARLIE: God – you sound like the light that failed!

HARRY: I said I'd try – you carping swine!

CHARLIE: I've had twenty years of your moaning, mate; and for once I crave a bright breezy statement: "Off they come tomorrow, Charlie!" That's what I crave – not the dingy inference of an oncoming Amen.

HARRY: *(Shouting.)* All right! Tomorrow. I'll unwrap tomorrow!

CHARLIE: *(Shouting.)* Thank you, Mummy!

HARRY: But no jibes, Charlie – like Monday's Pimple.

CHARLIE: Monday's what?

HARRY: Last Monday, that heat lump on top of my head. You said I looked like Cleopatra's titty.

CHARLIE: Oh? *(Pause.)* Oh yes.

HARRY: What're you laughing at?

CHARLIE: I wasn't. *(Pause.)* Monday's Pimple! Thought you'd created a new Doctor Series. "Monday's Pimple" starring Sherry Clade and...

HARRY: Shut your face! I've begged you! No jibes.

CHARLIE: *(Moving to his chair and sitting; purposefully calm.)* As you will, dear. As you will. Just discard the Maharajah stint; I'll be happy.

(There is a pause.)

HARRY: I appreciate you're trying shock tactics, Charlie.

CHARLIE: It's nothing. Nothing. Doesn't matter.

HARRY: *(Moving C.)* Yes it does. I must convince myself the World looks into my eyes; not at my skin. Damn it! I'll do it! I'll face them. I'll take up me comb, scissors and me clippers...

CHARLIE: You'll what! I beg yours, dear! You're not stepping into this shop, Harry. A bald hair stylist! You must be empty inside as well, thank you and hello the unemployed benefit.

HARRY: But where shall I go?

CHARLIE: Upstairs, dear. Up the kitchen flue. I don't care; but not in here with your wretched affliction.

HARRY: *(Moving above him to the window.)* You're horrid! You're inhuman; monstrous.

CHARLIE: Oh yes. Lovely. And how am I supposed to offer a bottle of shampoo or a nice friction massage? "Bluddyell," they'll say, "is that what happened to *him*?"

HARRY: *(Crossing above CHARLIE to C.)* The devil have you, Charlie Dyer! Rotten tormentor.

CHARLIE: Yes, I should rub a dub; here's us with a stock room of hair restorer – ten bob a go including the dropper; and you, Cleopatra's Titty, in the next chair. What! There's a nice ta-ta for a cold morning on the Left Bank!

HARRY: *(Sitting in his chair.)* Oh God!

CHARLIE: Your clipping days are over, dear.

HARRY: I'll die.

CHARLIE: *(Rising and putting his mug on the basin L.)* You and your one-legged men with wall eyes! *(Moving C.)* Be polite as you wish, you never find 'em in the Royal Ballet, do you?

HARRY: I'll swallow the stock room gas. Sniff it till I'm gone.

CHARLIE: *(Moving L of HARRY.)* I'm asking if you find knock-knee'd men in the Royal Ballet?

HARRY: *(Shouting.)* No. No. No. *(He rises and moves away R.)*

CHARLIE: Then there you have it, dear, haven't you. There you have it. So what with me and me magistrates, and you and your alopecia, we'll have a right happy Tonsorium, shan't we!

(HARRY bursts into tears and flings himself to the ground, sobbing bitterly. CHARLIE flops into his chair.)

I reckon I'll write a pantomime. *(He nods.)* Write a pantomime and call it "Noddy in Hell".

CURTAIN

ACT II

The same. Some hours later.

Outside, street lamps still shine but the sun is rising. A neon light is flashing somewhere. A lonely lorry lumbers up a distant hill.

When the CURTAIN rises, CHARLIE is discovered sitting on the floor C, his back against his chair. He is wearing pyjamas, with a shawl around his shoulders. Steps sound on the stairs. The shop door opens. HARRY enters in his dressing gown and pyjamas, and carrying CHARLIE's dressing gown. He switches on the lights and moves, blinking and yawning, to CHARLIE C. He hands CHARLIE the dressing gown.

HARRY: Why don't you come back to bed? You'll catch cold in your bones, sitting on the floor. You'll get piles.

CHARLIE: D'you know, Harry, you should write poetry for anniversary cards. You have such a silver flow of oratory. You could bring a new delicacy to contemporary literature: "Dearest Grandma, Full of Smiles. A Happy Birthday to your Piles!"

HARRY: It isn't half late. Long past dawn. Have you been weeping again?

CHARLIE: Oh belt up! What're you doing – working up an Agony Column? Feel like a fly in a milk bottle: can't breathe without *you* clucking round the brim. I'm in trouble so I'm the teensy-weeniest bit sad. It's natural, isn't it?

HARRY: Oh yes.

CHARLIE: Mental met-man! Checking if I'm damp or dry.

HARRY: Sorry.

CHARLIE: Oh, I'm worried a bit, that's all. It's not what you've done that counts – it's the way they describe it. And I'm petrified they'll – well, you know what they said about you when you had that scout troop.

HARRY: Oh well, they just used to ask if I was married, you see, Ch –...

CHARLIE: Yes, yes, that's what I mean. And with me being artistic...! See the old Judge up there. They'll crucify me, Harry.

(HARRY goes and sits in his chair.)

Everyone free from stain except Dirty Charlie. The way that copper'll paint me, I'll have asked him for a kiss in the bargain. And I'm innocent, Harry. As God's my witness, I did it for a gag.

HARRY: There's a new law – consenting males or something.

CHARLIE: Oh God help us all and Oscar Wilde! I was on Ed Chryslar's knee: he's as butch as Kong, dear. Been married to half Charing Cross Road. I need no laws. Need no laws.

HARRY: No. No, but I thought – you know – I mean – won't Ed Chryslar speak for you?

CHARLIE: They hate getting mixed, you see. Oh yes, I've um – rung three times; and heard a click! He's living with Sherry Clade. Lovely girl. I was in a show with her.

HARRY: Go to their house.

CHARLIE: Mm, I'll see Archy SeIder before the day. Archy'll give me some help. He's my agent, Archy SeIder.

HARRY: Has been for twenty years.

CHARLIE: Yes.

HARRY: Oh well, you've much to be thankful for.

CHARLIE: Oh yes! What! If I fell head first in a bog you'd say me shoes were clean.

HARRY: I mean you've had a good life and...

CHARLIE: What're you doing – laying me out? Laying me out, are you?

HARRY: No: I'm admiring you for having lived to the full, that's all.

CHARLIE: Off me own bat, mate. Nobody's helped me.

HARRY: Possibly not. You know, you talk about goldfish bowls...

CHARLIE: Goldfish bowls? Goldfish bowls? Who talks about goldfish bowls? *I* don't talk about goldfish bowls.

HARRY: I hadn't finished, dear.

CHARLIE: Working up a new fetish, are you? New fetish?

HARRY: *(Rising and moving to the bench.)* Oh suit yourself – going to be clever. *(He picks up a newspaper which has been folded at the crossword.)*

CHARLIE: Wilting under me badinage, then? On the wilting stint?

HARRY: *(Vaguely sulking.)* Nope. *(Muttering.)* Horoscope. Horoscope... *(He wanders up C.)*

CHARLIE: You what?

HARRY: It's a clue. *(He searches through the shelves up C.)* Seen my dictionary, Charlie? .

CHARLIE: That novelty thing from a cracker?

HARRY: *(Moving to the shelves down L.)* It was Margie's – my sister's. *(He searches in the shelves and cupboards L.)*

CHARLIE: Not surprised: it hasn't a single filthy word. I was checking yesterday.

(HARRY moves an antique deed-box from the cupboard.)

Mind me box! *(He jumps up, flings the shawl on the bench, and takes the box from HARRY.)* Full of me mother's mementoes, this. *(Crossing R.)* History! History, it is. *(He puts it on the stool.)*

HARRY: *(Discovering his pocket dictionary at the back of the cupboard.)* Ah! *(Then .)* There's a bottle at the back here. *(He produces a bottle of gin.)*

CHARLIE: *(Hurrying L.)* Bluddyell! *(He snatches the bottle.)*

HARRY: It's the one Ronnie Unsworth sent for my birthday.

CHARLIE: Many happy returns! Get the glasses!

HARRY: *(Taking two tumblers from the shelf L.)* You might well grab! It's more yours – the money you've spent on him.

CHARLIE: Belt up nagging! Disc jockey this; Harry Unsworth that! Give me a kiss, I'll tell you who's peculiar! Ho, ho, ha, ha!

(HARRY holds the glasses and CHARLIE pours two tots of gin. CHARLIE then knocks his back.)

HARRY: *(Toasting.)* All the best, Charlie, love. Hope everything works out well. *(He sees CHARLIE knocking back his gin, shrugs to himself and drinks. He then picks up his dictionary and sits in his own chair.)*

(CHARLIE puts on his dressing gown.)

Now – Horoscope. It'll say if it's Greek here – Horo – Hig – Hol – Hoopoe.

CHARLIE: *(Moving C.)* Hoopoe! What in great thumping charity's Hoopoe?

HARRY: Er – Hoopoe. South European bird with variegated plumage and large erectile crest.

CHARLIE: Filthy beast! *(He grabs the dictionary and throws it aside. Then he gives HARRY the gin bottle and goes to the stool. He puts his glass on the basin, takes the box, and sits on the stool.)* All me mother's little treasures in here. Look at this. *(He holds up a book, open, with a crushed flower within it.)* A crushed rose in her Golden Treasury. A feathery crushed rose from Yesterday.

HARRY: *(Putting the newspaper beside his chair.)* Always detested me – your mother.

CHARLIE: *(Brandishing the book.)* Nineteen-O-Something-
or-Other she filed a frail flower. *(He pops the rose back.)*
Twittering, giggling and pretty; look at her now! A
ninety-year-old walnut. *(He rises, takes the glass and box to
his own chair.)* If her head was filleted, she'd look like a
rusty prune. Oh, the sad, sad shrivelled bitch. There's
but one blessing, mate! She's past worrying about
hormones – male, female or variegated. I reckon that
hoopoe's as queer as a coot, anyhow.

(He sits, with the box on his lap.)

HARRY: That's how the aborigines do them.

CHARLIE: Do who?

HARRY: Shrunken heads. They sort of fillet them and stuff hot
pebbles through the earholes.

CHARLIE: Urrgh, you sadistic madam!

HARRY: Talented people, aborigines.

CHARLIE: Aborigines! We're discussing my mother. Do you
mind! Twit! God, me mind boggles at how that veiny
grizzled bag was once a twittering nymph from whose
pure little womb I... *(His lips quiver.)* Oh, Harry... !

HARRY: Yes, I only wish she understood me better.

CHARLIE: Too late now. Bones cracking; tissues rotten; mind
gone. She didn't know me last time I went. Did I tell
you?

HARRY: *(Rising to fill CHARLIE's glass; nodding.)* Smelly thing –
growing old. *(He sits again.)*

CHARLIE: "Hello, dear," I said. "Hello," I said; but she just
munched her gums; dribbling spit and a lump of puddin,
on her chin. Lips all puckered and tuckered like a badly
stitched haggis. *(He gulps gin and wipes his eyes on his
sleeve.)* Screwing me up, this gin is. *(He sniffs.)* I'd been
there half-an-hour; then all of a sudden: "Who are you?"
she said. *"Who are you!"* What! "I'm your bloody son,

dear," I said. "Silly old bitch," I said; but it didn't move her. Eyes all faded. Mental block, d'you see, Harry. *(He begins to weep.)* She h-hates me so m-much...

HARRY: *(Rising to C, with the bottle and his glass.)* It was her who made you, Charlie.

CHARLIE: Yes! Yes, mate! And I reckon God's punishing me, Harry.

HARRY: *(Ponderously.)* Maybe He's punishing your mother.

(CHARLIE pauses a second, impressed.)

CHARLIE: That was very deep, Harry. Very deep; and quite beautiful. And she's been expensive, Harry. Cost pounds a week, my mother has, you know. Pounds. It's been difficult. Difficult. I mean, if I'd had a few quid to myself, I might've got married again.

HARRY: Oh, be logical.

CHARLIE: What d'you mean – logical! How dare you! How bloody dare you! Many a woman I could've had. Many! I'm not like you – with your antennas and scout poles! Hundreds of women I could've had.

HARRY: *(Filling CHARLIE's glass.)* Yes: well, you had your mother.

CHARLIE: Too true. Oh Harry – it's an awful place she's in. The Matron'd put the wind up Edgar Poe's ghost. I'm afraid to visit after dark. I really am. Stairs creakin' like groanin' monks; draughts shrieking up the chain mail. And you remember that vulture in the hall? Glass case? I'll swear it's not dead. Crossed pikes over the lavatory doors. I was in agony me last visit – I wouldn't "go", dear. Pull the chain in that place – drop in a snake pit!

HARRY: *(Putting the bottle on the basin R, then sitting in his chair.)* Yes, you'd think they'd splosh a bit of sunny pink. I did my mother's room from top to bottom.

CHARLIE: Rubbing it in, are you? On the triumphant stint? *(Tenderly, he opens the poetry book.)* My mother – who once pressed a rose.

> "So softly creeps the warming light
> And gently fades the loving night..."

Bastard! (He rises, hurls the book down and stamps on it.) Blasted pressed rose! Pandora's blasted box! *(He puts the box on the table down L.)* What am I going to tell her? I'll – I'll miss me visiting days! *(He returns to his chair and sits.)* What am I going to say? "Guess what, Mummy! They're calling me a puff!"

HARRY: It'll only be a fine, Charlie.

CHARLIE: You think so? You really think so?

HARRY: At very most.

CHARLIE: Yes. *(He nods.)* Yes. *(And then .)* A fine. You've a blasted cheek: *I'm innocent.* Oh, God help us all and Oscar Wilde.

HARRY: *(After a pause.)* 1 sometimes wonder what they say – you know, Charlie – upstairs – when my sister calls on *my* mother.

CHARLIE: Ten whole days!

HARRY: I can just hear Margie yacking: "How old's Harry, now, Mum?" she'd say: and Mum'd say: "I don't know. How old is he?"

CHARLIE: Circular conversation.

HARRY: But that's how they talk.

CHARLIE: Should live in a turret!

HARRY: Yes; and Margie'd say: "He's old enough to've been married." Then she'd say – I can just hear her – "Mum, d'you think he's – he's a..." *(He bites his lip and grips the arms of his chair. He sits awhile, shaking his head.)*

CHARLIE: What time're you due in Court? Eh? Eh? This is *my* wake, not yours, dear.

HARRY: I'd go to Court ten times to have your hair.

CHARLIE: And I'd swap every lock to stay out, mate. What! That's where God's so clever, you see.

HARRY: When 1 was over at Margie's last year...

CHARLIE: Oh, is she back again?

HARRY: No, listen: 1 had, well, a dreadful experience. 1 was bouncing their little boy on my knee. Gurgling; chubby. He's about three. And he threw his arms round my neck and pushed his peanut nose in my ear; and, oh Charlie, 1 couldn't help hugging and squeezing him. "Oh you darling darling thing," I whispered. Then it all happened.

CHARLIE: Happened? What happened?

HARRY: The baby – began screaming. Wouldn't stop. Then Dick ran in – all diddems and waddems. "What did you do?" he said. "What did you do?" His voice thick and accusing: face all over the front of his head. *(He sighs deeply.)* How can you tell a man with hairs curling over his collar that you only wanted someone to hug; something to love?

CHARLIE: Kids! You get 'em on lease; get 'em on lease until they're fourteen; then they shove on tight trousers, and accuse you of stunting their growth!

HARRY: But to have a baby...

CHARLIE: You're maudlin. Your eyeballs 're frothing with gin. 1 can hear 'em bubblin'.

HARRY: Ah but, Charlie. If you and me – you know, if we could've had a little lad of our own. All our own, to teach and cherish. Oh, I'd've loved him till he popped.

CHARLIE: Babies! The one reason we like 'em, they're the only living creatures more stupid than us.

HARRY: They wouldn't let us, anyhow. Such a shame; but they wouldn't give a baby to our kind.

CHARLIE: *(Rising and going down L.)* Speak for yourself, mate! *I've had one. (He looks in his mother's box.)* Hello! *(He finds something in the box.)* Lock of hair! Good God, it's mine! A lock of me infant's hair! *(His lips quiver.)* Oh-oh, H-Harry! Worms're crawling in me stomach and screaming for those dear dead days! *(He slams the box lid.)* Bastard! Bastard! Hate me mother! Always did!

HARRY: *(Rising, picking up the bottle, and filling both glasses.)* There, there. Have another gin. *(He puts the bottle on the floor and holds out CHARLIE's glass.)*

CHARLIE: Oh my poor shrivelled Mammie – stuck in that resting place of elephants. Antique bucks and bitches, all death trumpets and grey sagging leather. One camp bed; one cane chair; and eight cubic feet for dying in. *I'm pulling her out!* Today! *Today!* Back she comes!

HARRY: Pulling her out where?

CHARLIE: *(Moving C.)* Here. Home, where she belongs. *(He takes his tumbler.)*

HARRY: In *my* home?

CHARLIE: She'll not bother you. Fit in upstairs.

HARRY: *My* mother's fitted up there.

CHARLIE: Yes. Lovely. Lovely. Muck in together. Lovely.

HARRY: Oogh, you're clever, you are, Charlie. Break me heart, fill me with gin; then creep your mother into me attic.

CHARLIE: Have another gin...

HARRY: You're not stuffin *my* house with sagging leather. *(He moves below his chair.)*

CHARLIE: Well! This is it, then. What! The treacherous stint! Treacherous stint.

HARRY: Afraid to tell Matron why you won't be visiting Mummy for ninety days.

CHARLIE: Oh! Got me inside now! There's a nice monocle for a blind man, you bastard!

HARRY: The Matron was a very nice lady, *I* thought.

CHARLIE: Bats of a feather, dear! Bats of a feather!

HARRY: Now you listen, Charlie... *(He holds CHARLIE's arm.)*

(CHARLIE shakes him off.)

CHARLIE: No I won't. Get off! *(He moves round his chair to up c.)*

HARRY: Never face me, will you! Rotten fungus-face! Never admit the truth...

CHARLIE: *(Singing in a loud voice, to the* Hallelujah Chorus.*)* Alopecia! Alopecia! Alopecia. Alopecia. Al-o-o-pecia!

(HARRY sits in his chair, setting his face into an expression oj disinterest. CHARLIE prances round him, pointing at the bandages.)

Alopecia! Alopecia! Alopecia. Alopecia. Oh alo-p-pe-cia. Etc. Etc.

(He collapses, laughing, into his chair.)

HARRY: Thimble of gin and you're up the Monument. I don't know.

CHARLIE: God! For a parade of swans in a lane of diamonds instead of paper boats in dirty buckets. D'you know, Harry, I haven't one single memory. Did you know? Not a single memory. Never stick. Never stick. My only flash of life is a day at school: there was a real ram of a lad, and his sister. We called her Milky Moe because she was overdeveloped. She was six. And Milky Moe stole my frog.

HARRY: Milky Moe did what?

CHARLIE: Stole my frog, dear. My frog. A-wooing-go and all that. I worshipped that frog. I'll bet there's something deeply psychological if I could but lay my fingers upon it.

HARRY: *(Rising and picking up the bottle.)* I could lend you memories; but you never listen.

CHARLIE: Goldfish bowls! Goldfish bowls, you said; a damn lie! I never mentioned them.

HARRY: Ah, but you said you felt like a fly in a milk bottle. And I feel like a fly on a goldfish bowl, d'you see? Sort of walking *outside the world* all day. Worse! I'm worse. *(He puts the bottle on the basin R.)* A fly probably knows he can't get his feet wet and enjoys his stroll. I long to wet me feet and haven't the guts to jump in!

CHARLIE: *(Impressed.)* You dig up some interesting rubbish on the quiet, Harry. *(He rises and, taking his glass, moves L to the mirror.)*

HARRY: Thank you. Oh, I was always the strange one. *(Sitting in his chair.)* Unhappy child, I was, Charlie. It was all this "Vive la difference!" hoo-hah. I remember, as a lad at the swimming baths the women with their bodies all private, on one side; and the men on another side. A funny business, it seemed. I'd look at *my* body; and I'd think there's a woman next door, looking at hers. And I couldn't, you know, get me thoughts untangled.

CHARLIE: *(Gazing at himself in the mirror.)* I might dye my hair, I think. Make me look less evil at the trial.

HARRY: Life's just two great separate piles. You're supposed to whoop from one to the other; and if God's given you enough bounce, Bob's your uncle. If not – you're right in it! I've tried hard, Charlie. Once I wore long scarves; rubbed me hands when anyone mentioned beer; and chuckled in dark brown if they asked "Are you courting?" Till I was thirty-five I did that; then I started getting headaches. Just those two piles; nothing down the middle.

CHARLIE: *(Still at the mirror.)* I have a kindly face in the main.

HARRY: I had a talk with a parson once; you know, a vicar – for advice. But he was more embarrassed than me, Charlie. Couldn't shuffle his face into the right expression. Looked as though he'd just noticed horns on the curate! Made me a cup of tea and told me about his eight children. Eight children, he had!

CHARLIE: Typical! Tells you to put your trust in God: then dashes to the manse for a bunk-up! *(He soothes wrinkles round his eyes, then considers himself.)* 'Course, *I* look well in clerical grey. Me best bet, that is, looking hen-pecked and married. By hell – I could take Cassy. *(He swings round.)* "*This is my daughter, Gentlemen of the Jury*" – Your Honour! M'Lud! *Meet my daughter.* That'd shake 'em. Ha! *(Then his triumphant mood fades.)* But how'd I tell her in the first place? Going to be a trial saying "How-do" without ploughing straight into a homosexual homily or whatever-it-is.

HARRY: It's a nuisance, the whole thing. *(He rises, puts his glass on the basin R, and moves C.)* I'm very sorry about it all, Charlie.

CHARLIE: Yes; but, I mean, if she turned out to be a wowzer, Harry. You know, mate: a real lush babe. And I could say *That is mine!* I *made* that!

HARRY: Marvellous, Charlie!

CHARLIE: *(Moving LC.)* Aw...! I should be that lucky, dear! What! I'll bet she's threaded on twine; face like a whippet; and a bosom like two monocles on a monk's bench. *(He flops into his chair.)*

(HARRY moves to him and stands behind, patting his shoulders.)

HARRY: If it's any help, Charlie – I'm frightened, too.

CHARLIE: Thanks. *(Then, as though surprised.)* It *is* a help, Harry. A nice help – you breast-fed gnat! *(He shakes his head, then lowers it.)* If only – if only it hadn't happened,

Harry. If only it hadn't happened. If only I could stare at me shoes – and blur me eyes – and find myself in a different safe moment when I look up... *(For several seconds he stares at his shoes.)*

(HARRY keeps patting his shoulders.)

(Whispers.) It's not happening – not happening. I'm not here... *(Then he looks up; but it's the same old moment! He probes his fists deep into his stomach and groans.)*

HARRY: They can't do anything if you're innocent, Charlie. And you *are* innocent – aren't you – Charlie!

CHARLIE: Do I have to grovel for you, too? Humiliate myself here as well ?

HARRY: No. No, Charlie; but we'll get by somehow.

CHARLIE: I hope so, mate. *(He reaches up and pats HARRY's hand.)* By God, I hope so.

HARRY: What starts it! *(Moving R and picking up the bottle and his glass.)* Oogh, it's frustrating! What makes a violinist – a genius – a great lover! They say it's hormones; and I detest the whole damn system, I do! You know – *(Moving C and pouring two more gins.)* – they showed films – in one of those operating shows on television – they showed you moving pictures of the whole reproductive system of a ferret.

CHARLIE: In opposition to the London Palladium, was it?

HARRY: Ha... No, it was fascinating, really. All these magnified actually moving photographs. And a ferret – or was it a horse?

CHARLIE: Easily mistaken.

HARRY: No, it was a horse, this bit. Fantastic, dear! Actual photographs of a thousand squiggling *things. Carnal things* – squiggling inside this horse...!

CHARLIE: Urrrgh, you obscene hag!

HARRY: But it's true, Charlie. *Things*! *In us*! Oh I hate life. Hate it! Hate the whole dirty business...

CHARLIE: Oh belt up, will you! Will you belt up! You twisted umbilicologist! *I'm trying to forget*!

(HARRY moves R and puts the bottle back on the basin.)

My head's corrugated and there's cannon balls rumbling over the ruts. I've enough to worry on the outside without you medicating all over the... *(He stops. Then slowly, worriedly.)* Harry, you don't think – I mean – I've seen it in the newspapers: "Remanded for a medical report". *(His voice shakes.)* Harry, you don't suppose they'll remand me for – f-for anything like that?

(HARRY moves to him.)

HARRY: No, Charlie. No, no, no, love.

CHARLIE: Remanded for a medical report.

HARRY: Oh, that's a different situation...

(CHARLIE looks small, old and pathetic.)

CHARLIE: Old Charlie, hair stylist and one-time dramatic actor, was this morning rem-m-... *(He covers his mouth.)*

(Now HARRY clears his throat and puts on a business-like air.)

HARRY: I'll leave you alone, Charlie, when...

(But before HARRY can finish his sentence, CHARLIE grabs his arm anxiously.)

CHARLIE: No! Guddelpus no! *Not alone.*

HARRY: When Cassy comes, I meant.

CHARLIE: Oh! Oh yes – thanks.

HARRY: And be quite honest, Charlie. Tell her the truth; and ask if she'll come to Court with you. It's your best bet.

CHARLIE: Yes. Yes, it is. *(He surges into fresh optimism.)* And perhaps we could sprinkle a few of your mother's knick-knacks around: even down here, as well. You know, everywhere.

HARRY: Knick-knacks, um...

CHARLIE: Well, I shan't be seeing my mother until afterwards, or I'd've borrowed her stuff.

HARRY: No, take my mother's.

CHARLIE: Good. Good. Thanks, love. *(He turns his chair to face his mirror.)* I might grow a moustache by next Wednesday.

HARRY: Charlie! Why?

CHARLIE: Mm?

HARRY: Why d'you want mother's knick-knacks?

CHARLIE: Um – *(He shrugs.)* – oh, you're not connected with the theatre. A dramatic touch.

HARRY: Tell me, Charlie!

CHARLIE: Well – she'll imagine I'm living with some fancy woman instead of... *(He stops.)*

HARRY: Instead of me.

CHARLIE: It's better than have her wondering things, isn't it! Oh who cares!

HARRY: *(Moving above CHARLIE's chair to the window.)* I care! I blasted care! You're making me a~a filthy shadow. Shall I scratch my name off the window, too?

CHARLIE: What're you going up for?

HARRY: *(Crossing back above CHARLIE to C.)* I'm fed up being hidden and elbowed into shadows to suit you!

CHARLIE: Tragic stint? Tragic stint?

HARRY: The one person in life I'd've liked to meet would be Cassy. She's the one *real* thing – the only *real* thing about you, Charlie.

CHARLIE: It was your own suggestion. "I'll go out", you said.

HARRY: To suit you! By hell! A lifetime of bolstering *you*; feeding *you*; worrying for you. And now you're too damned ashamed to have Cassy meet me – *in my own home.*

CHARLIE: I'll tell you about the time I had digs in Clitheroe...

HARRY: When have you ever bolstered *me*? *(Moving below his own chair.)* Never! Never once said "Well done" or "Nice work, Harry!"

CHARLIE: Last Monday I said the porridge was nice. I distinctly remember: "Christ, Harry," I said, "this is beautiful porridge".

HARRY: Porridge! When have you ever made me feel big?

CHARLIE: Maybe you're not big, mate! Maybe you're not. *(He regrets this immediately.)* I was joking, dear. *(He rises and moves to HARRY.)*

HARRY: *(Quietly.)* You weren't, Charlie. That's the whole point. Deep down you believe you're better than me. Don't you! Answer me, Charlie.

CHARLIE: Well, I am artistic, aren't I. I mean – I can't help what I feel, can I? *(He moves away C.)*

HARRY: Well blast you! You and your whole cruel West End sardonic bunch. You balance your own failures by insulting others. That's why you get at me with your quick wit and ready repartee: you use me as a kind of staircase between flops.

CHARLIE: And up you and your good-will-to-men for a start! What! I should... Goddam it, you're standing there, on that very spot, doing exactly what you're accusing me of! Grinding me down as you've done for twenty years.

HARRY: Oh, I'll not have that!

CHARLIE: Not have it! Not have it! *You've got it!*

HARRY: Yes – well – who says you're so big? What've you ever done? And anyway, how d'you know she's yours, dear?

CHARLIE: How what? Who? *She? She who?*

(HARRY regrets now.)

HARRY: Nothing.

CHARLIE: Talking about Cassy, weren't we! Another vicious goose from my ever-loving mate! It's like living on a vampire's pogo stick.

HARRY: Charlie...

CHARLIE: She's *mine*, mine, you bastard!

HARRY: Yes. Of course she is.

CHARLIE: God, you're clever! Just slide 'em in, don't you: the little doubt, beautifully cooked, just slipped under me eyeballs to scratch and niggle.

HARRY: Well *she*'ll not like you dragging Cassy into it. What if she said...

CHARLIE: A lie! A lie!

HARRY: *(Heatedly.)* Maybe; but *I* shouldn't want a daughter dragged through the mud, alibi-ing her father's – lovelife. "No thank you," I'd say. "She's not his!" I'd say. "He's just a bum I married for convenience," I'd say. Any lie I'd tell if I were Cassy's mother.

CHARLIE: *(Shouting.)* Well, you're bloody not – much to your creeping disappointment, Mrs Lactating Harriet Leeds!

(HARRY shrugs. CHARLIE glowers for a few seconds, then plucks his lip thoughtfully.)

It'd be slander, that would. *I* did the asking. *Me*! Real masher in those days, I was. Oogh, I was so beautiful it hurt.

HARRY: Yes, Charlie...

CHARLIE: Back line of the chorus, *her*.

HARRY: Yes, I know.

CHARLIE: Snapped me fingers. Snapped me fingers and she
was grovelling...

HARRY: Charlie – Cassy was premature; it only needs some
legal bigwig to uncover...

CHARLIE: Bigwig! Bigwig! Where're they trying me, House
o' Lords? 'S'only a tiddly Case for God's sake. Local
butcher they'll have on the bench; he won't postpone to
search Somerset-blasted-House. Cassy's *mine*. *Mine*. She
has my – my eyes – my... Anyhow, me and the Old Sow
were having it off for years, boy, years!

HARRY: *(Quietly.)* You weren't, Charlie. You weren't.

CHARLIE: You wide-hipped belly-grubber...! *(His intended
blistering volley stops suddenly. The words choke him. He covers
his face; and his voice is low, near to tears.)* Did you *have* to
bring it up? Could've done without this one. W-wouldn't
involve me own daughter, I wouldn't: just a quick idea
to keep me going. *(He raises his face; eyes closed, hands
clenched.)* If only I'd been certain all those years ago. If
only I'd been sure, I might never have... Oh, if only it
hadn't happened. *(To HARRY; ferociously.)* You! Hope your
nipples drop off as well! Dog in the manger? You've got
hyenas!

*(HARRY shrugs into his chair. CHARLIE strides over, towering
above him.)*

Oh, I see it now. Anything to whittle me to *your* level.
(Shouting cruelly.) I bet you pray nights: "Please God
make Charlie small like me!"

(HARRY leans forward, his head in his hands.)

HARRY: Oh – I feel dizzy, I think.

CHARLIE: Here we go! The "oh-me-heart" stint; the
"coughing-me-last-hours" stint! Ask yourself honestly:

are you or are you not happy when there's no excitement in my letters – no television work – nothing in me pocket – and nowhere to go except this hairy-aired brilliantine fleapit? Well?

HARRY: *(Leaning his head back.)* I suppose I have been jealous sometimes but...

CHARLIE: She admits it! Right out? *(He moves to the window, and turns.)* I suppose you realize you copy me? You copy me, you're so envious.

HARRY: When you live close to someone, you can't... *(He shakes his head; he is unable to finish.)*

CHARLIE: Why don't you fight back? What're you so silent for? On our pale and wan stint, are we?

HARRY: Have you ever wondered if I'm really here?

CHARLIE: Oh guddelpus! That's the second time today! *You're there!* Slap bang *there*!

HARRY: Like your agent, Archy SeIder?

CHARLIE: *(Moving below his chair.)* You what!

HARRY: You've no agent, Charlie.

CHARLIE: Ha! *(Blustering.)* Oh rich! Oh...

HARRY: Archy – spelled with a Y. Usually it's spelled I E. Isn't it?

(CHARLIE is still and apprehensive. He says nothing. HARRY takes a paper from his pocket.)

And d'you remember those postcards when you were away? When you used to write about the great play you were starring in; and your co-star Sherry Clade?

CHARLIE: A great voice! Sherry Clade could reach a top C above...

HARRY: And your famous impresario D'Arcy Relshe; and the society woman who worshipped you, Sherly Drace? And Chard Seerly and so on?

CHARLIE: Doing a biography, are you? Biography?

HARRY: I jotted all those names on a paper. I got to thinking, you see. What a funny name, I thought – Chard Seerly; and Archy Selder with a Y; and D'Arcy Relshe! *(He rises to face CHARLIE.)* They all spell Charles Dyer. *They're all you, Charlie!* You've never mentioned anyone who isn't an anagram of Charles Dyer.

(CHARLIE sits in his chair and swings to face the mirror L. HARRY tosses the paper in front of him. CHARLIE clears his throat.)

CHARLIE: Bit dumb if you've only just found out.

HARRY: I've known for years.

CHARLIE: I once started a play, Harry. Never finished it – thought it might be an idea to have everyone's names the same as mine.

HARRY: Charlie, what – I've always been frightened – what were you really doing? During those two years?

CHARLIE: I-I was, um – selling encyclopedias.

HARRY: *(In relief.)* Is that all?

CHARLIE: I need excitement, Harry. Haven't your guts to be ordinary, Harry. Hate being ordinary.

HARRY: Yes – but I want to know, Charlie. Was there anything else?

CHARLIE: Um – I was on me own, Harry, d'you see. You kicked me out and...

HARRY: You walked out.

CHARLIE: Well, anyway, I landed in doss houses some nights. Oh, horrid dumps I slept in. Wasn't much commission on 'cyclopedias; and I like a good laundry for me shirts, dear. And one day, I thought – What! I might as well be in – *(He pushes these words through his pride.)* – be in jail. Ha ha.

HARRY: Oh my God!

CHARLIE: I'm glad it's out, Harry. Been choking me – ever since the summons. Had to tell someone.

HARRY: *(Wearily.)* It'll be on your records.

CHARLIE: *(With a flash of spirit.)* Think you're telling me? Do you? Why d'you think me head's been corrugated all night?

HARRY: What was the charge?

CHARLIE: I got thirty days...

HARRY: The charge, Charlie! As though I didn't know...

CHARLIE: I did nothing, Harry. It was a pub near this air force base. Youngsters marching with their proud chests – and I was kipping in this cellar at four bob a night – old meths drinkers belching in me ears. And you know I enjoy a bit of comfort. I – I just asked a lad if I could come back to camp with him.

(HARRY covers his face and groans.)

CHARLIE: *(Vehemently.)* There but for the grace of God, Harry! There but for the Grace! By hell, if ever I finish me great play, I'll name the villain after meself: to prove I've a spit o' faith in humanity; to show there's one living Twit with enough compassion not to label others 'you people' or 'them' or 'those'; to prove I've enough humility to travel under any label – any label – without shame. *(Tiny voice.)* I never do anything, you know that, Harry. God's Truth, I never do anything. I just like clean, new people; fresh and young. Like being *near* them.

(Now we realize, gradually, that HARRY is the stronger of the partnership. It is CHARLIE who is the weak one.)

HARRY: You met him in a pub.

CHARLIE: Yes. Well, I'd kept 'em laughing. Kept 'em in stitches with me tales, Harry. I've a vibrant personality. I'm an old pro – they'd never heard some of my songs. But – I was all alone at closing time.

HARRY: This finishes us! *(He moves down R.)*

CHARLIE: Aw – it's ten years ago.

HARRY: You promised. *Promised.* Said you'd only drink at home. Swore on my mother's upstairs Bible.

CHARLIE: We'd had a row, hadn't we! Your Bible didn't count on the two years.

HARRY: So hundreds of policemen surrounded the air force base and drummed lies in the Judge's ear.

CHARLIE: *(Nodding.)* Ninety days – for nothing.

HARRY: Two years was your sentence, Charlie, wasn't it! Two years.

CHARLIE: *(Nodding.)* Nearly – nearly. Um, they let you out early, d' you see. If you're good.

HARRY: *(Flaming into anger.)* D'you never consider anyone? Never think of *my* shame? Staying with you! People pointing at us – at the two weirdies, Harry and Charlie. And there's nothing wrong with me. There's nothing wrong, and I have to suffer the strain because of *you.*

CHARLIE: You what! I should rub a dub. I mean, you're hardly Ghenkis Khan, are you, dear! So don't waft your feathers too high – we'll see your corsets.

(HARRY moves up C and rests his head against the wall.)

HARRY: Oh, I feel wretched. What with you, and the gin, and being up all night. This finishes us. Finished! I warned you. Warned you and warned you.

(There is a pause.)

CHARLIE: And to think my father was a parson! Although they say he was odd, too. Left me mother – he wrote "You wear it!" on his collar and flung it in the hall. Very religious man, he was. Very religious. A Muswell Hill Adventist or something, he was.

(HARRY, on a sudden thought, takes a pencil from the shelf C, picks up the folded newspaper and writes on it.)

HARRY: *(Muttering.)* Ed Chryslar... *(He ticks off the letters, then looks up.)* So you were sitting on Ed Chryslar's knee for a gag!

CHARLIE: I know. I know. Ed Chryslar spells me own name, as well. *(Quickly, before Harry can start on questions.)* No use asking me, Harry, because I can't remember.

(HARRY sits in his chair.)

Drunk. Drunk. When I came to, they were dragging me out of the Club; said I was masquerading – masquerading as a w-woman. Young copper, scuffing me. Fell on me knees, I did; scraped them all. I was clutching his legs; everyone watching. "Please, *please*," I said, "you'll ruin my life, son." I'd've been in the Maria except for this nice Inspector. "Up you get, Dad," he said – calling me "dad" now! But he told this young copper. What! "Can't you see this is a gentleman," he said.

HARRY: Did he hell!

CHARLIE: *(After a pause.)* He said something quite nice.

HARRY: Yeah – what?

CHARLIE: "Don't be greedy," he said. "Send the poor old bugger home." *(He sits nodding his head for a moment or two in silence.)* "He might do himself in or something." the young copper said. And the Inspector said: "Save time if he did." Yes, I've known three who did, Harry. Three who did. A problem, it is. Such a problem. Ruined me marriage, you know.

HARRY: Oh, it was the Problem, was it? I see.

CHARLIE: *(With a shrug.)* May as well take all offences into con-sideration – Ladies and Gentlemen of the Jury. She was a good person, really, the Old Sow. A good old sow, she was. If I'd had one spot of tact... What! I've as much tact as a stallion's buttock.

HARRY: And I'm twice as ugly.

CHARLIE: I know she was only after a baby. I know that. It was me body, mate! Me health and beauty. But Um, I wish I was back with her. *(He shakes his head.)* Wish she hadn't kicked me out.

HARRY: Do you! Do you really! Oh well.

(It is daybreak. HARRY busies himself in the shop. He pushes up a large electric switch – perhaps the neon sign or burglar alarm. Then he moves R and picks up the towel from the basin.)

Once, when Mother needed a hairnet, I popped to the chemist on the corner; and – you know – I didn't like asking for it.

CHARLIE: So I should damn well think! A barber asking a chemist for an 'airnet! Sounds like a code word.

HARRY: Well, we'd sold out. Anyway, I said it was for my wife. And ever after they kept asking: "How's your wife?" Oh, I loved it. Loved having a wife.

(We hear a milkman's shout off; bottles rattle on the step.)

It made me belong; like a parson in swim trunks getting a slap on the back.

CHARLIE: You're not twisted: you're hexagonal.

(HARRY switches off the room lights up c, then picks up the towel from the basin L and moves to the stock room door.)

HARRY: But now I'm nothing again. *(He turns.)* Have you ever thought about my name, Charlie?

CHARLIE: Bluddyell! What're you flogging this line for? On the psycho stint, are we? Psycho stint? Your name's Harry Leeds, mate. Very pretty.

HARRY: It spells Charles Dyer.

(HARRY exits into the stock room. CHARLIE sits quite still for a second or so, then rises to pick up the newspaper and pencil and sits scribbling on it, muttering.)

CHARLIE: H-A-R-R-Y – Harry. L-E-E... *(Having written the name, he crosses out the letters one by one.)*

(HARRY enters from the stock room with a sweeping brush.)

HARRY: Fantastic, isn't it!

CHARLIE: There's no C.

HARRY: C for Chris, my middle name. You know I always sign myself Harry C. Leeds. *(He moves above his chair.)*

CHARLIE: *(Rising.)* Oogh, *you must be joking*! *(He backs away L.)* See me inventing you! Pull the other one!

HARRY: *(Moving C.)* Strange though, eh?

(CHARLIE backs away from him again.)

CHARLIE: I'm getting out! Out, mate! By God, you're right we're finished. I'm getting out before little goblins start running up me arm. *(He runs to the lobby, brings on a suitcase, puts it on the arms of his chair, and starts collecting his personal combs, brushes, clippers, scissors and things from the cupboard and shelf down L and putting them into it.)* I'll go to a bloody nunnery! *(Then he pours the contents of his mother's souvenir box into the case.)* I only make beautiful people. Beautiful people, I make. Like nice fresh sweet-smelling things, I do. You! You're shrivelled and ordinary, mate! Accuse me of creating you! What! I'm no impressionist. I'd have someone with black curls. Black curls I'd have. I should rub a dub. *(He stops, breathless, and looks at HARRY.)* Nothing to say? Nothing to say, then? I'm going, you know. Walking out that door.

(HARRY moves up R to sweep stray clippings into a pile on the floor.)

HARRY: Terrible terrible thing – not to be liked; not to be even necessary. If a great big nozzle sucked me into oblivion, there isn't a clock'd stop ticking.

CHARLIE: Got to make yourself not care, mate: like me.

HARRY: Trouble with our sort, you're never left with anyone. 'S' an impossibility. It's an empty room when whatever friends you've got go first.

CHARLIE: Twenty years I've stuck by you.

HARRY: Well, it's been warm; and I've taught you a trade, Charlie.

CHARLIE: Oh, I'll put that in "Spotlight". Leading Character Actor. Shakespeare a Speciality. Able to Drive – And Trim Nostrils!

(HARRY, having swept the dusty fluff on to a newspaper, empties it into the waste bin up R. Then he takes his brush to the stock room door.)

HARRY: It's not one-sided, Charlie: because I need somebody all my own. And after all, I can't see a "little me" in *you*, Charlie. Can't watch *you* growing up. A shame, it is: we could've walked through the years together. Blame's on both sides, I suppose.

(HARRY exits into the stock room, closing the door. After a second, CHARLIE moves to the stock room door. He calls quietly.)

CHARLIE: Harry! Harry? Aren't you going to wait for me, then? Harry? Oh, suit yourself. *(There is no reply. He kicks the door and moves to the gin bottle. It is empty.)* Dry as a camel's chamber pot! *(He tosses the bottle into the waste bin, then looks about him, scratching his neck and licking his lips.)* Hair restorer! I'll have a tot of that. *(He shouts at the stock room.)* And maybe I'll die; then you'll be sorry! *(He rummages in the cupboard down L and produces a bottle of hair restorer. Shouting.)*

I'm having hair restorer! D'you hear – you ramshackle old queen! *(To himself.)* But he's not. He's nice and ordinary; that's the trouble. *(He clenches his teeth.)* God, I wish I could say straight out: "Harry, you're a beautiful old stick, love." Why can't I say it? Why can't I say: "Please Harry, keep me room warm for when I come out of jail"? *(He turns to face the stock room. Firmly, he calls.)*

Harry, Harry! will you… *(But he cannot make his lips finish the sentence. Instead, he puts the bottle to his lips and gulps the hair restorer – which he immediately spits into the basin L.)* Uurrgh! I'll die *next* week, I think. *(For a while he leans on the wash basin, peering at himself in the mirror.)* Harry C. Leeds. Harry C. Leeds. Fantastic! I never planned that one! Don't say I'm seeing 'em as well! *(He swings away from the mirror and shouts.)* Of course you're there! I wouldn't invent a shrivelled mirage like you, mate! *(To himself.)* Oh no! I'd have someone with black curls and slim hips. *(He shouts.)* You there, mate! You're horrible and concrete! *(He moves to the stock room door; bangs on it.)* D'you hear? Harry? Harry! *(He tries the door knob. Seemingly it is locked.)* Harry, what're you doing? *(He bangs on the door.)* Damn fool – locking the door! Harry! You all right, Harry? Harry! Harry, what've you done?

(CHARLIE's shouting and banging becomes frantic. He pushes against the door. It begins to open – slowly, as though something heavy were lying on the other side. Eventually, CHARLIE forces his way in. HARRY is lying on the floor. CHARLIE steps over him and out of sight. We hear him coughing – then the sound of breaking glass. CHARLIE returns in view and drags HARRY into the shop, below the chair RC.)

(In tears.) Fool! Bloody fool! *(He applies artificial respiration.)* Not alone, Harry. Don't leave me. Not alone – not alone – not alone, Harry. *(He listens at HARRY's chest, then tries more hopefully.)* You bastard. Can't be so bad! Holding out for the kiss of life, mate? What! I should rub a dub. Back, boy. Come back. Harry, come back, love!

(HARRY starts coughing. He pushes CHARLIE away and sits up.)

HARRY: What – what're you – what're you doing?

(CHARLIE sits back, panting from his exertions.)

CHARLIE: Oh lovely! Yes! I've only strained me heart saving you. I could kill you for this.

HARRY: Oogh, I'm feeling better.

CHARLIE: Mean slut-faced puff, trying to leave me! You'll never live this down, dear. Never. Why d'you do it?

HARRY: I did nothing, Charlie.

CHARLIE: I'll never feel safe with you. Spend me life watching you.

HARRY: Just – sort of red came upwards across my eyes. And d'you know, Charlie. I heard my own bang as I hit the floor.

(CHARLIE rises and moves to the stock room.)

CHARLIE: Squatting there with your small talk. I might've had the coppers in. Coppers, mate!

HARRY: What coppers?

CHARLIE: *(Closing the stock room door.)* What coppers? What coppers?

(He stops at a sudden thought. Opening the door again, he sniffs the atmosphere.)

HARRY: No need for sniffing. I checked the jet.

CHARLIE: It's in! *(Accusingly.)* That flame's still in.

HARRY: 'Course it is.

CHARLIE: But – but I've just smashed that window.

HARRY: Silly bee! Wasn't it funny, though: touch of blood pressure, I bet; I had it once before, remember?

(HARRY moves to the stock room. CHARLIE steadies himself against his chair, leaning over it.)

I'm back to myself now. All fine... *(He notices CHARLIE.)* Here! What is it, dear?

CHARLIE: The shock, mate! The shock. Phewsh! *(He slides to his knees.)*

HARRY: Charlie! *You thought* – oh hell!

CHARLIE: Yes – *that's* where I thought you'd gone. Disappointed now.

HARRY: *(Kneeling beside him.)* Bit of a shock, was it?

CHARLIE: *(Nodding.)* I thought, um – thought I was on me own, Harry. And um, I think you're... *(He tries again.)* I think you're *(And in a whisper.)* – a beautiful old stick.

(But HARRY does not hear CHARLIE's whisper.)

HARRY: Pardon? I couldn't hear, Charlie.

CHARLIE: Oh belt up, and give me breathing space. *(He elbows HARRY away.)*

HARRY: *(Rising.)* Very well, Charlie. You take things easy, eh? Here, shall we close today?

CHARLIE: Could do.

HARRY: Have the day off, eh? Right you are.

(HARRY exits into the stock room.)

CHARLIE: *(To himself.)* Too old for this lark! God, what would I have done? Nowhere to go! And what about *him*? *(He looks upwards.)* There! I thought about him, God. I did think about *him*, God-mate. *(He closes his eyes, speaking fervently; and – even though, in seconds hence, he'll be back to the same old CHARLIE – in this one moment, CHARLIE believes in God; and by God he prays!.)* Oh God, make me remember this. Please God, just help me at the Assizes, as well; and I'll never think another foul thing. And I'll make Harry diet and see a doctor. And may Mum drop dead and everyone leave me alone if I don't remember this lesson. *I will. I will.* Please Jesus, make me remember how lonely people are; little cripples and little blind folks. Amen.

HARRY: *(Off.)* Charlie, don't be cruel!

(CHARLIE is startled. He opens his eyes fearfully, thinking God has spoken.)

CHARLIE: Who said that!

(HARRY enters, wearing a thin, bad wig. He moves L of his chair and waits apprehensively, as CHARLIE turns to look. CHARLIE rises from his knees. He tries hard – but cannot enthuse; instead, he seems cowed and subdued.)

Ah! It's quite nice. Very nice, Harry.

HARRY: Well, I warned you, didn't I?

CHARLIE: No! It's nice. It's um – didn't they have any other colours?

HARRY: My hair *was* black. Curly black. Thick black curls, I had.

CHARLIE: Oh yes. Yes, I know. I know.

HARRY: You don't like it. Knew you wouldn't. Said so.

CHARLIE: I do. I do, Harry.

HARRY: Oh, I hate you like this – all subdued and holy. Are you staying for ever like this?

CHARLIE: Well... *(He shrugs.)*

HARRY: I'd rather you said one of your cruel thrusts. Go on, Charlie. Get it off your chest.

CHARLIE: The wig's fine, dear. Fine. *(He moves away LC.)*

HARRY: *(Following CHARLIE and holding his arm.)* Charlie! Charlie, I don't mind. Tell me the truth. Be yourself!

(CHARLIE stops and looks over his shoulder at HARRY's head. That old evil relish glimmers.)

CHARLIE: Where're you... *(He stops.)*

HARRY: Don't stop, Charlie! Straight out!

CHARLIE: Where're you going to keep it at night – in a cage?

HARRY: Yes, that's you! That's my old You. Go on! More. Tell me more.

CHARLIE: Well – it looks like you've spat ink on a hot boiled egg!

(But this is too much for HARRY.)

HARRY: Oh, you bastard! You're horrid and vicious.

CHARLIE: You asked me! Asked me!

HARRY: You and your pretty hair! I hope it erupts from your scalp. Erupts and erupts – until the shop's an overgrown church hassock with taps; and you in the middle, clawing for life. Hair in your eyes, through your ears, and up your bloody jumper! *(He flops into his chair.)*

(CHARLIE moves to him.)

CHARLIE: You going to wear that when you meet Cassy?

HARRY: Meet her?

CHARLIE: Might as well. Anything for peace. *(He walks round HARRY, surveying the wig.)* Could be worse. Pleasantly surprised, I am. It sort of grows on you. Sorry, Harry. *(He moves L and considers himself in the mirror. A night has passed, and his chin is shadowed again.)*

(We hear creaking on the staircase. They look upwards. HARRY rises and rushes to listen; but CHARLIE just rubs his chin at the mirror.)

HARRY: Ta-ta, Sexy!

CHARLIE sits in his chair. HARRY bustles to his record-player and puts on the Hallelujah Chorus*; then he goes to his basin R, takes his little bowl and soap, and begins lathering CHARLIE's face as –*

– the CURTAIN falls.